WANTED

Cultural Frames, Framing Culture

Robert Newman, Editor

WANTED

The Outlaw in
American Visual Culture

RACHEL HALL

UNIVERSITY OF VIRGINIA PRESS

Charlottesville and London

University of Virginia Press
© 2009 by the Rector and Visitors of the University of Virginia
All rights reserved
Printed in the United States of America on acid-free paper

First published 2009

1 3 5 7 9 8 6 4 2

Library of Congress Cataloging-in-Publication Data

Hall, Rachel, 1974–
  Wanted : the outlaw in American visual culture / Rachel Hall.
    p.   cm. — (Cultural frames, framing culture)
  Includes bibliographical references and index.
  ISBN 978-0-8139-2855-5 (cloth : alk. paper) — ISBN
978-0-8139-2856-2 (pbk. : alk. paper)
    1. Wanted posters—United States. 2. Violence in popular
culture—United States. I. Title. II. Title: Outlaw in American
visual culture.
NC1849.W36H35 2009
364.973022'2—dc22

                                                        2009013581

For my parents

Certain assemblages of power (pouvoir) require the production of a face, others do not.

—Gilles Deleuze and Felix Guattari,
A Thousand Plateaus

CONTENTS

ILLUSTRATIONS

ACKNOWLEDGMENTS

DURING THE COURSE OF WRITING THIS BOOK, I MOVED from Chapel Hill to Syracuse to Baton Rouge. In the process I made friends, incurred debts, and relied on the kindness of strangers.

This book began at the University of North Carolina (UNC), where I benefited from the brilliance and generosity of many mentors: Lawrence Grossberg, James Hevia, Victoria E. Johnson, D. Soyini Madison, Carol Mavor, John McGowan, and Della Pollock. Several of my peers at UNC contributed to this work by reading, offering suggestions, and providing food and fun: Lisa Calvente, Rivka Eisner, Ian Finseth, Jules Odendahl, and Greg Siegel. Others provided much-needed support during those first few years out of graduate school: Kelly Gates, Frances Guerin, Craig Robertson, Gil Rodman, Brian Rusted, Ted Striphas, and Barbie Zelizer.

This project benefited from the expertise and interest of a lively group of research librarians: Rachel Canada in the Manuscripts Department of Wilson Library at UNC, Jeffrey M. Flannery in the Manuscripts Department at the Library of Congress, the reference librarians in the Motion Picture and Television Reading Room at the Library of Congress, and John Fox at the FBI.

Two talented editors, Sharon Willis and Michael Bowman, helped get the book rolling by offering early assistance on revising chapters of the dissertation for publication as articles.

Four readers of my work deserve special thanks for

slogging through multiple drafts and offering timely encouragement along the way: Stephanie Hawkins, Dustin Howes, Phaedra Pezzullo, and Della Pollock.

Thanks to everyone at the University of Virginia Press. I especially want to thank Cathie Brettschneider, who first recognized promise in my work. I also want to thank my reviewers at Virginia for their smart and demanding suggestions. Finally, I wish thank the cultural studies editor at Virginia, Robert Newman, for his enthusiastic support and incisive comments.

My colleagues at Syracuse were good to me during my brief time there. Thanks to Bernadette Calafell, Ann Clarke, Doug DuBois, Diane Grimes, Roger Hallas, Amos Kiewe, Judith Meighan, and Kendall Phillips.

Many thanks and much love to my colleagues, graduate students, and friends at Louisiana State University. I have benefited from the steady support of my chair, Renee Edwards, and deans Guillermo Ferreyra and Robin Roberts. The university provided two summer stipends that were crucial to the completion of this project. Hearty thanks to friends Dana Berkowitz, Michael and Ruth Bowman, Tracy Stephenson Shaffer, and Trish Suchy for keeping me afloat through two difficult years.

Thanks to my family for their consistent shows of support and interest in my work: Sarah, Dan, Red, Charles, and Kim Hall; Mary Ruth and Carroll Kendall; Sara and Lou Thompson; Bill and Frances Dowers; Sharon Hall and Bill Houpt; Janet Howes and Ed Guisdala; Joann Stoddardt; Marylin Kelly; and the Howes clan: Brandon, Randy, Colleen, Jason, Corey, Russ, and Sue.

Thanks to Erica Rothman for sharing her warm intelligence and rich store of metaphors. Without her help, this project would not have been possible.

Finally, a very special thanks to the two people who never doubted the value of this project or my ability to realize it: Phaedra Pezzullo and Dustin Howes. Phaedra is a dear friend who enriches my life every time I get a chance to connect with her. Dustin is a sharp, patient, and unselfish partner. I am lucky to be with him.

Portions of chapter 2 were previously published in my essay "Missing Dolly, Mourning Slavery: The Slave Notice as Keepsake," *Camera Obscura* 61 (April 2006).

WANTED

INTRODUCTION

The Making of the Vigilante Viewer

IN PERSONAL ADVERTISEMENTS OR "WANT ADS," THE word *wanted* communicates some lack on the part of the ad's author: our band has no drummer, there is no one home between 2:30 and 5:30 to watch my kids, I have no one to go to the movies with me, I haven't had sex in a while, I do not have the help I need around the house, I lack the physical strength and mobility to shop for myself. It communicates something that someone needs or desires. *Wanted* functions, therefore, both instrumentally and expressively, although the expressive aspect varies widely from one want ad or personal ad to the next.

Not so for the police. In wanted posters issued by law enforcement professionals, the trick is to communicate what the police want without admitting lack, dependence, or least of all desire. Puffed up and serious, printed in all caps, and often appearing in boldface type, WANTED stands down connotations of desire, lack, and vulnerability by signaling danger. The wanted poster aspires to be a sober, realist text that can make things happen.[1] But the word *wanted,* no matter how big and bold the type, introduces uncertainty into the text regarding whether or not the authorities will get what they want. In the space between the mug shot and the word, the poster visualizes the limits of authoritative speech: look and see the ones who got away. In a populace that has for the most part relinquished violent force to the authorities, this is cause for alarm. The outlaw's wanted status demonstrates a lack or temporary failure of police power. In posters put out by the authorities, WANTED signals an emergency and attempts to transfer that sense of emergency to the public. While the wanted poster announces that something has gone awry, it reads more like a command issued to the citizenry than an admission of police failure. Perhaps this is because the word *wanted* carries the memory of a federal mandate.

The first known wanted poster was issued by the Department of Justice and called for the capture of a notorious draft dodger.[2] Hollywood images of the nineteenth-century frontier not withstanding, prior to the issuance of this circular, there was no such thing as a wanted poster. Reward notices had been around since the sixteenth century, but they would not have been called "wanted posters" because they led with the dollar amount offered for the capture of the fugitive. Early on, reward notices used the word in order to explain to readers what the fugitive was wanted for, as in "wanted for burglary," "wanted for swindling," or "wanted for forgery." In the Pinkerton collection, which houses a selection of reward notices issued by the country's first national detective agency during the late nineteenth and early twentieth centuries, it is not until about 1924 that the word *wanted* begins to appear in agency posters.[3] Even then *wanted* is not the poster's heading, but merely listed below the mug shot as the rationale for the poster's call to capture. The primary objective of the wanted poster for draft dodger Grover Bergdoll is not to communicate a reward offer but to label the fugitive from military service anti-American. This shift in the notice's function, from designating crimes to marking a traitor, can be tracked through a slight wartime modification in the grammar of the reward notice: *wanted for* dodging the draft becomes *wanted by* the United States.[4]

It is difficult to know exactly how or why WANTED replaced the offer of a dollar reward as the typical poster's heading. But given that this development happened during World War I, one wonders if the word's rise to the top of the poster is not somehow attributable to its prominence in war propaganda from the period.[5] Is it possible that "wanted by" in the Bergdoll notice is a restatement of the claim made on Bergdoll and other

WANTED BY THE UNITED STATES

GROVER C. BERGDOLL

NOTORIOUS DRAFT EVADER and DESERTER wanted by the UNITED STATES AUTHORITIES AT PHILADELPHIA, PA., on charge of wilfully evading the SELECTIVE SERVICE ACT.

Grover C. Bergdoll, a member of a wealthy Philadelphia family, interested in the Bergdoll Brewing Company, left Philadelphia in August or September, 1917, since which time he has been traveling extensively throughout the country. It is believed that he is constantly on the move, accompanied by a male companion. He is an expert automobile driver and aviator, and delights in exploiting his ability in both lines. He is flashy and dramatic—a lavish spender of money. When entertaining, he displays a large roll of notes.

Description:—Five feet four inches in height; dark hair, brushed pompadour; scar on face; teeth stained by constant chewing of tobacco; heavy set figure; weight about 175 lbs.; affects brown clothing and shoes.

This man is a serious offender against the laws of the United States, and his arrest is earnestly desired by the military authorities. Every effort should be put forth by Federal and State Officers to bring about his apprehension. An appeal is made to all patriotic citizens to co-operate with the authorities in effecting his arrest. In the event of his apprehension, please detain him and wire or telephone full particulars to the undersigned, or to the representative of the Department of Justice at Philadelphia.

Office of U. S. Attorney
Telephone Walnut 2213

FRANCIS FISHER KANE,
United States Attorney for the Eastern District of Penna.,
Philadelphia, Penna.

Office of Dept. of Justice
Telephone Walnut 2844

TODD DANIEL,
Acting Local Agent of Department of Justice, Philadelphia, Pa.

Wanted poster for Grover Bergdoll, 1917. (Courtesy Federal Bureau of Investigation, Washington, D.C.)

recruits by the words "wanted for" in James Montgomery Flagg's famous World War I image of Uncle Sam? First published as the cover for the July 6, 1916, issue of *Leslie's Weekly,* with the title "What Are You Doing for Preparedness?" Flagg's painting, according to the artist himself, went on to become "the most famous poster in the world." Indeed, over four million copies were printed between 1917 and 1918, as the United States entered World War I.[6]

While there are many important differences between Flagg's propaganda poster and the wanted poster for Grover Bergdoll, this book is about what they share in common. Both posters visualize the difference between what the state wants and what it has not got. They communicate the federal government's physical lack of bodies—the body of a draft dodger in the first case and the bodies of potential recruits in the second. However, the blood lust expressed in the wanted and recruitment posters is carefully encoded and authorized: in the first case through strict adherence to the visual codes of police sobriety and in the second case through the personification of the nation as the reader's elder. William J. T. Mitchell reminds us that Uncle Sam developed out of nineteenth-century British caricatures of Yankee Doodle and notes the continued importance of Uncle Sam's appearance as a "character" to the visual rhetoric of recruitment: "What this real and imagined nation lacks is meat—bodies and blood—and what it sends to obtain them is a hollow man, a meat supplier, or perhaps just an artist. The contemporary model for the Uncle Sam poster, as it turns out, was James Montgomery Flagg himself" (38). The federal government persuades more citizens to sacrifice their bodies to the nation, while hiding death behind full-color, mass-produced illustrations of an aged, avuncular mascot. By representing patriotic duty through the figure of the potential recruit's uncle rather than his father, the poster mobilizes the family metaphor, thereby alluding to a paternalistic economy of obedience to the father and sacrifice for the family, even as the displacement from father to uncle softens the material claim Uncle Sam is making on the nation's "sons."

But as Mitchell notes, Uncle Sam's appearance is not merely ideological: "The 'disembodiment' of his mass-produced image is countered by its concrete embodiment and location *as picture* in relation to recruiting stations (and the bodies of real recruits) all over the nation" (38). The recruitment poster evinces a high-stakes social network made up of bodies and

I Want You for the U.S. Army, 1917. (Courtesy Library
of Congress, Prints and Photographs Division;
illustration by James Montgomery Flagg)

images: "the bodies of real recruits" and images of Uncle Sam, which compel citizens to sacrifice their bodies for the sake of the nation.[7] Likewise, the wanted poster for Grover Bergdoll installs networks of peer surveillance and moral obligation composed of the bodies of real readers and Bergdoll's image, which prompts citizens to become informants, thereby facilitating Bergdoll's capture or surrender. The wanted poster for the draft dodger is an ambitious text. It aspires to force a reunion between representation and reality, image and referent, Bergdoll's portrait and his body. But it needs the public's help to make this happen.

There is, of course, a crucial difference between Uncle Sam's direct address, which orders recruits to report for duty, and the wanted poster for Grover Bergdoll, which encourages citizens to help the federal government discipline those who fail to report. The recruitment poster hopes to draw the nation's readers together in a spirit of common cause, whereas the wanted poster performs a filtering function. By displaying Grover Berg-doll's portrait, it visually separates the draft dodger from the rest of the citizenry. Its business with him is physical, but its business with the public is visual. The wanted poster wants to produce a mode of spectatorship that I call the vigilante viewer. I borrow this formulation from John Caldwell, who uses the term to describe the particular brand of interactivity that characterizes television viewers of programs like *America's Most Wanted:* "The activated televisual consumer was now . . . a vigilante—a televisual bounty hunter energized by patriotic appeals to American morality, law and order" (260). For Caldwell the vigilante viewer refers to a historically spe-cific version of televisual interactivity first cultivated during the late twen-tieth century in "the well-oiled and lucrative cable ghettos of Christian television," which later rose to prominence with the Fox Network's intro-duction of reality television in the late 1980s.

In this book I demonstrate that the vigilante viewer was a long time in the making and that media other than television, such as broadsides, news-paper advertisements, the rogues' gallery, and wanted and missing posters, have cultivated an interactive mode of spectatorship closely related in spirit, if not in time, to Caldwell's televisual bounty hunter. The practice of putting outlaws on display and the interactive modes of spectatorship that this practice elicits are not late-twentieth-century phenomena. It is more accurate to say that when the Fox Network introduced reality television, the late-twentieth-century vigilante viewer encountered outlaw displays in her living room, whereas the nineteenth-century city dweller had encountered criminal portraits in the rogues' gallery, and the mid-twentieth-century reader had scanned the faces of the wanted at the post office. There are of course significant formal, contextual, and historical differences among these viewing scenarios, which I address in subsequent chapters. But just as compelling is the durability of a particular mode of spectatorship, its politics, and its affect, as it migrates across a range of media.

To begin with, the vigilante viewer is *not* a vigilante. At best, she exchanges information for a cash reward, which is a very different transaction from the one the bounty hunter makes when he captures and delivers the fugitive's body, "dead or alive," to the authorities. In fact, the performance of this type of vigilance requires that one relinquish violent force to the authorities. "Vigilante" modifies the viewer's practices of looking, rather than her physical interactions with outlaws. In visual cultures of crime the vigilante viewer's eye functions like the bounty hunter's gun once did. It is the viewer's weapon and her protection in a world plagued by violent crime. It is what the vigilante viewer can use to help make the world a safer place.

The vigilante viewer is not a vigilante insofar as his visual commitment to keep an eye out is simultaneously an act of submission to police authority. In looking at images of "real" outlaws provided by the police, the vigilante viewer plays the role of layperson and perhaps even helpmate or cheerleader to the professionals. For him outlaw displays simultaneously reinforce the necessity of the police and the importance of the public's cooperation. Ostensibly a call to join the manhunt, the wanted poster actually positions the reader as a spectator.[8] By this I mean to say that most readers understand that they are not part of the action, which transpires without them. This is true even and especially in the case of the professional wanted posters issued by the police. While there are law-and-order subcultures in which armchair detectives crave the chance to make a positive identification, the average passerby does not really want a live encounter with the outlaw. If he stops to read the wanted poster, it is because he wants to see "what a real outlaw looks like." For the vigilante viewer the wanted poster is less a genuine exhortation to join the manhunt than a mildly successful prompt to banal acts of visual consumption and episodic fantasies of violence. To admit this is not to deny that the wanted poster "works." Anyone who has watched an episode of *America's Most Wanted* knows that the practice of publicly displaying outlaws has helped the police to catch an impressive number of criminals. But the wanted poster's iconic status does not turn on the fact that some very small portion of the poster's audience occasionally knows the whereabouts of a wanted fugitive and phones in a tip.

Vigilante indicates a practice of looking that extends beyond the text of the wanted poster and the context of a particular reading or viewing situation. The vigilante viewer sets him- or herself apart from less enthusiastic patriots by carrying the lessons of outlaw consumption into daily life. For the vigilante viewer vigilance means sustained awareness of the endless parade of real outlaws, who signify the reality of crime. Vigilance also describes the ancillary effects such practices of looking have on the spectator's everyday routines, corporeal relationship to various geographies, and visual interactions with others. Significantly, the vigilante viewer is not confined to urban settings or major metropolitan areas of the United States. The vigilante spirit thrives in rural and suburban areas where the relative threat of violent crime is lower and therefore requires a more imaginative viewer and a greater investment on his or her part. The vigilante viewer consumes national images of crime and imaginatively transports the threat of violent crime into his or her geography, routines, and experiences. Outlaw displays glamorize and repudiate the outlaw as exceptional or abnormal, the better to frighten and excite vigilante viewers with his possible encroachment on safe, familiar, and mundane locales.

By proffering a model of spectatorship, I do not mean to suggest that vigilante viewers are a homogeneous group or that the practice of looking hard is uniform across individuals and contexts. Actual vigilante viewers exist on a continuum that runs from the super vigilante viewer who sees President George W. Bush plant the flag at Ground Zero and promptly enlists, to the home viewer who phones in a tip to *America's Most Wanted* that leads to the capture of a fugitive, all the way down to the person who reads wanted posters in the post office much like she would the tabloids at home—for the brief and pleasurable escape they afford from the tedium of errands. While the post office reader might be considered relatively passive in comparison to a reader-turned-informant or a viewer-turned-soldier, it is likely that her reading practice still has important implications. That is, the act of regularly consuming images of outlaws likely has ancillary effects on the viewer's behavior, including her voting record; attitudes regarding police work; ideas about guilt and innocence; imagined geography of safety and danger; and interactions with friends, relatives, and strangers.

Finally, *vigilante* refers to the affective economy that accompanies this mode of spectatorship. The act of publicly displaying the outlaw communicates an economic (and ultimately physical) threat to the viewer's well-being. The outlaw's embodiment of illegitimate desires positions readers of the poster as his future victims. In this sense the wanted poster says not only that the authorities want this man but also that this man might want *you*, he might covet *your* family, he might come after what *you* have. Understood as a visual technology for producing fear, the wanted poster's ultimate object is the vigilante viewer's body. At its most potent the wanted poster effectively transfers a death threat issued by the police to the viewer via the outlaw's frozen stare.

The vigilante viewer defends him- or herself by returning the outlaw's gaze. Looking hard provides an opportunity for the moralistic consumer to burn off stores of economic anxiety. Discipline is not, therefore, a straightforward matter of learning from the outlaw's bad example to exercise self-restraint. Rather, it has to do with submitting to a visual culture of productive consumption. The wanted poster cultivates the comparative look of consumer culture as a psychic defense against the guilt and anxiety produced by the unequal distribution of wealth in capitalist societies. Consuming the outlaw's image constitutes a form of expenditure for the vigilante viewer. The mug shot provides the channel by which discipline momentarily moves away from the viewer, where it gets recharged by the outlaw's minor spectacle of dangerousness, the better to serve as a prompt to the viewer's self-congratulatory practices of legitimate consumption. Hence the visual pleasure produced by celebrity mug shots, in particular, which offer the tragic appeal of the fallen star coupled with the reassurance that the vigilante viewer's life is more productive, if less glamorous.

Looking hard reinforces the consumer's alienation, even as it promises to make everyday life less banal. For the alienated consumer crime and violence, in particular, take on a reality quotient that ordinary life lacks. The mall becomes a threatened and possibly adventurous space for the informed vigilante viewer, who knows there could be a child molester or two lurking among the throngs of family shoppers. At the end of the day, the vigilante viewer does not really want contact with the child molester, only the fantasy of violence and moral taboo that he embodies. Ultimately, she will leave the business of catching the creep to the professionals. Indeed, the primary visual trick of the wanted poster is its use of outlaw imagery to signify the necessity of professional policing. Framed by the wanted poster, the villain's image divides the world into those in need of protection from him and those capable of providing that protection.

The wanted poster invites performances of what feminists have termed "the protection scenario." Susan Jeffords describes the protection scenario as that which is "established through three categories that stand in unstable conjunction with one another: the protected or victim, the threat or villain, and the protector or hero" (770).[9] It does not matter if the vigilante viewer is a man or a woman. Either way, the vigilante viewer plays the feminine part of the protected to the police officer's protector. The act of posting outlaws legitimates the masculinized violence of the state and law enforcement and treats the world as a feminized space that could ideally be sealed off from threat, like a family's home might be protected from unwanted intruders, a woman's body rendered impenetrable, or a child sheltered from the dangers and disappointments of the world. These gendered geographies of fear and security are borrowed from the frontier imaginary, where vigilante violence is considered a proportional response to innocence (defined as prospective property) lost. Outlaw displays want viewers to play the part of the protected such that the act of consuming said displays reinforces the innocence of the viewer's modes of acquisition as compared to the outlaw's.

While official outlaw displays reflect police power, they also make a point of appealing to the democratic citizen's right to property and to a standing police force that would protect the interests of the "upstanding" or propertied. Framed by the wanted poster, the mug shot carries a particularly strong, if implicit, connection to the family portrait, with its investment in the sanctity of the home. This is because the wanted poster periodically produces and repeatedly stimulates an imagined geography of dangerousness inherited from the frontier. In the social and psychic geography of American culture, the wanted poster occupies the border that separates home from the external dangers that threaten its sanctity. As such, the wanted poster is not only an expression of the law but also a gendered cultural form for the ritual reenactment of property relations. Within this visual economy family is both a place—a point of orientation for material longing—and a body of sentiment in whose name individuals strive for more or violently defend what is already theirs. The idea of family gives a moral sheen to the desperation of striving for material wealth and the violence used to defend private property, as well as racially exclusive communities and practices. The paternalistic habit of imagining threats to family and the violence used to guard the home come to seem not merely rational but also righteous.

The wanted poster, in particular, reinforces the vigilante viewer's faith in possessive individualism through public displays of outlaws, defined as those individuals who have forfeited the right to self-possession to become the property of the state.[10] Within societies that organize social relations according to property rights and subscribe to the tenets of possessive individualism, and for which the possessive individual forms the basic social and economic unit, the ultimate punishment is to strip the outlaw of his individualism, understood as his right to possess material wealth and, most profoundly, his right to self-possession. In other words, within such societies identity takes the form of personal property. Liberty, too, or the individual's free will, is understood as a form of property, such that the body becomes an instrument for depriving the individual of said liberty and the face serves to picture, announce, and rationalize that act of forceful deprivation.[11]

The wanted poster is dramatic and possesses the charged temporality of social demotion insofar as it marks the outlaw as the future property of the state, which is tantamount to stripping him of his right to act according to his will. The outlaw's change in status is visually communicated through the shift from the visual conventions of proper portraiture to those of the mug shot. Whereas the proper portrait possesses depth and features the individual in a bust or a three-quarter shot, signifying interiority (free will) and heart (humanity), the mug shot pictures the absence of interiority through the collapse of depth and dehumanizes the outlaw by cropping his head sharply off from the rest of his body.

Noting the visual currency between honorific and repressive genres of portraiture, photographer and art historian Allan Sekula argues that the mug shot ought to be understood as the other side of the proper portrait: "To the extent that bourgeois order depends upon the systematic defense of social relations based on private property, to the extent that the legal basis of the self lies in the model of property rights, in what has been termed 'possessive individualism,' every proper portrait has its lurking, objectifying inverse in the files of the police" (7). Indeed, the mug shot is meaningful in relation to family, school, army, and celebrity portraits. Like these other forms of portraiture, the mug shot places the individual within a larger currency of photographs and thereby positions the person pictured with respect to society as a whole.

In the United States the threat of turning a person into property reverberates with the history of slavery. The character of the bounty hunter, featured prominently and even comically in Westerns, is haunted by the figure of the slave hunter. And the image of the slave, born the property of a planter, haunts the image of the outlaw, whose punishment it is to become the property of the state. I do not speak metaphorically when I say that the slave serves as the forgotten body of reference for outlaws who have "earned" their punishments through criminal acts. The earliest known photographic reward notice manufactured in the United States was, in fact, a Civil War–era poster for a runaway slave. I examine this poster and its implications for the history of outlaw display at length in chapter 2. The fugitive slave's status teeters between guilt and innocence, depending on whether readers view her as a missing person or stolen property. As property she retains the innocence of the inanimate. A Yankee must have stolen her, the notice's author reasons. As a person she is guilty of abandoning her post and betraying the white family who used to own her.

Since the abolition of slavery the status of property has been reserved for two populations: outlaws and women-and-children. Perhaps this explains the striking formal similarities between wanted and missing posters and their broad cultural function as templates of guilt and innocence in the American imaginary. If the wanted poster reinforces possessive individualism by displaying those who have forfeited the right to self-possession to become the property of the state, then the missing notice reinforces possessive individualism by picturing the woman-child as the lost or stolen property of her parent(s). In other words, the missing notice is implicated in the ideology of the bourgeois family and the history of family law that defines women and children as the legal property and vulnerable charges of their husbands and fathers. In the frontier imaginary the father's role as protector is racialized. He must protect his claim and family from the encroaching wilderness and the natives who lie in wait there.[12]

Due to their uncanny capacity to frame persons as property, missing and wanted posters inadvertently function as cultural images of mortality. Missing notices picture the faces of children whose lives, the reader cannot help but assume, have been tragically cut short. Marita Sturken describes this reader's experience well: "These children," she writes, "who ask us to search for them look, in fact, already gone, marked by the mortality of the image. They appear arrested in previous time, unable to grow older. They offer moments of prior innocence that proclaim the end of that innocence" ("Image" 192–93). For Sturken the use of age-progression technologies in missing-child notices only sharpens our sense of the image as memorial, rather than as an instrument of identification and recovery. This technique for visualizing what a missing child might look like *now* is particularly cruel insofar as it can only ever show viewers an artificial, proximate future self for a child who appears to have no future.

The wanted poster, too, frames the fugitive within the grammar of life and death. Wanted: "Dead or Alive," the fugitive inhabits the "or"—the placeholder between "life" and "death"—but not for long. The wanted poster projects his death, either in the final shoot-out or in jail, where he may be put to death or left to rot. In *Homo Sacer* Georgio Agamben argues that the bandit is, like the wolf-man, a figure with liminal status.[13] He is someone who lives on the threshold between inclusion and exclusion, life and death. As the person banned from civilization, he is excluded from the peace guaranteed by community. He becomes the man without peace, one whom anyone may kill without committing homicide: "To ban someone is to say that anyone may harm him . . . or [that he] was even considered to be already dead" (104–5). The wanted poster aims to turn the fugitive's metaphoric capture by photography into the literal capture of his body by the police. This is not a matter of the health of the outlaw's spirit; rather, it concerns the business of recovering his body, "dead or alive," so that it might be subjected to punishment.

The wanted poster gives us access, therefore, to a founding contradiction of American society. The text employs the modern technique of individualization as a means of social control where identity becomes a form of property, pictured as the face. At the same time the text expresses the primitive desire to capture and punish the outlaw's body according to rituals of expulsion and regeneration. I adopt Carolyn Marvin and David Ingle's definition of "primitive" as describing those processes that construct the social from the body (4). In their study of totem ritual and the nation-state, Marvin and Ingle argue that blood sacrifice is a defining feature of American society. But Americans are not in the habit of thinking of themselves as engaged in rituals of blood sacrifice. Keeping the totem secret—we kill our own—requires vigilant compartmentalization. Every society must maintain a categorical distinction between rationalized forms of state-sponsored violence, characteristic of American police, juridical, and military practice, on the one hand, and the violence practiced by "primitive" individuals and societies, on the other. Marvin and Ingle write: "To group members (Americans), violence signifies the primitive, the Other of the border. Modern societies define themselves as essentially non-violent. By contrast, primitive societies are said to practice violence shamelessly. In popular mythology blood sacrifice is a feature of primitive societies, but not our own" (64). The wanted poster's blood lust is borne out by its formal and historical connections to war propaganda and recruitment posters, in particular, which call for citizens to sacrifice their bodies in the service of national interests.

The vigilante viewer typically responds to cultural images of emergency with fear, moral indignation, and patriotic fervor for law and order. And yet the same vigilante spirit stoked by the authorities is not entirely containable within the frames of law and order. The vigilante viewer's desire for images of crime and punishment may exceed the bounds of patriotism in order to produce other pleasures, derived from America's long-standing romance with the outlaw. Motivated by desire for danger, the vigilante viewer uses outlaw images to negotiate what historian Daniel Cohen refers to as "the darker contradictions of a moralistic consumer culture that alternately mandate[s] self-discipline and self-indulgence" (38). The wanted poster is particularly well suited to the moralistic consumer's visual work insofar as it belongs to the age of information, and yet, like the recruitment poster, it points to the power of a story sanctioned by death. Walter Benjamin writes: "What draws the reader to the novel is the hope of warming his shivering life with a death he reads about" (*Reflections* 101). A related, yet distinct, phenomenon draws the vigilante viewer to the wanted poster. The mug shot is a deadened image of the fugitive, but the viewer's knowledge that he is on the run renders the wanted poster a death-defying image, which may inspire desire, admiration, regret, or hatred.

In the U.S. context the wanted poster retains traces of romance and sadism. This fact points us to a significant difference between the French context, of which Michel Foucault wrote, and visual cultures of crime and punishment in the United States. In *Discipline and Punish* Foucault makes a compelling case that punishment has become "the most hidden part of the penal process" (9). "At the beginning of the nineteenth century," he writes, "the great spectacle of physical punishment disappeared; the tortured body was avoided; the theatrical representation of pain was excluded from punishment. The age of sobriety in punishment had begun" (14). Foucault theorizes this historical development as a shift from one visual culture of crime and punishment to another, from the age of spectacle to the age of surveillance (202).[14]

While I find Foucault's theory of power in the modern era useful in terms of describing the disciplinary function of professional outlaw displays, I do not accept his narrative of a wholesale transition from spectacle to surveillance in the history of crime and punishment. If the spectacular age of crime and punishment was over by the beginning of the nineteenth century, then why would Andy Warhol be moved, in the middle of the twentieth century, to use the mug shots of wanted criminals in his artwork, much as he had the celebrity portraits of cultural icons like Marilyn Monroe and Elvis Presley?[15] In the American context the wanted poster is an instrument of surveillance, but it is also a popular spectacle of dangerousness—not to mention a death threat issued by those with the institutional power to make good on their promises. Instead of a wholesale transition from spectacle to surveillance, the history of outlaw display offered here tracks a shift from spectacular live punishments and bodies in pain to the reigned-in everyday pleasures of visually consuming images of dangerousness and, perhaps just as important, serial promises of punishments aimed at someone else.[16]

In what follows I assign vernacular practices of fugitive display historical primacy and narrate the subsequent adoption and transformation of those practices by modern institutions. My methodological approach is informed by the work of the photo historian Geoffrey Batchen, who writes, "We have yet to see vernaculars being made the organizing principle of photography's history in general, yet to see a *vernacular* theory of photography being advanced" (59). While we tend to think of the wanted poster as a sober police text, vernacular fugitive displays reveal a textual tradition that is by no means dry. Runaway slave notices, in particular, offer the viewer a glimpse of a decidedly messier, more personal, and more explicitly violent tradition of communication. These texts express concern at the growing geographical distance between their authors and the fugitives they advertise. In so doing, they indirectly reference the former physical proximity of these two bodies, author and fugitive, and call for their violent reunion.

Later professional displays toned down the expressive violence characteristic of vernacular traditions by rendering the professional detective's relationship to the body marked for punishment in abstract terms. First, photographs of individual fugitives replaced typical illustrations of the fugitive body. Then, the modern fugitive was portrayed merely as head and shoulders, shrunk down to a size appropriate to the commodity form of the trading-card photograph. Next, the fugitive's body was fragmented, measured, and counted, such that it became a statistical body of information that spoke for or against him. Later, the fugitive's fingerprints joined his mug shot in police displays, where both demonstrated the state's hold on him (and every other individual, for that matter). The act of translating the body into a face was arguably the most crucial step in this process. The mug shot eschewed the body. In so doing, it pictured Western ideologies of difference between primitive and civilized acts of punishment, barbaric and rationalized forms of violence.

In the transition from vernacular to professional fugitive displays, the role of the spectator changed dramatically. For one thing, spectators no longer confronted the outlaw's image or description in a local community where they might be expected to interact with or physically apprehend the fugitive. Readers consumed fugitive displays authored by distant and absent authorities. Further, as the social and geographic distance between the professional authors of fugitive displays and lay readers increased, *vigilante* came to signify the viewer's practices of looking rather than his or her proximity to the fugitive's body or capacity to violently apprehend him. Fugitive displays became representations of police work as much if not more than calls for the reader to get involved in the manhunt. Ironically, as American police organizations claimed the work of fugitive apprehension for professionals only, they managed public perceptions about police work by playing to popular nostalgia for the vigilante violence of the frontier. As a result, American fugitive displays never lost their sadistic charge or flair for romance. And the vigilante viewer learned to negotiate the cotemporality of fugitive displays (at once modern and premodern) by cannibalizing the outlaws offered up to him or her in "sober" displays of police practice. In this exchange the outlaw became the vigilante viewer's alibi. He put a face on the primitive desires the vigilante viewer exercised in consuming him. The picture of dangerousness, he appeared to be the source of the violence that characterized the vigilante viewer's look.

Chapter 1 provides a prehistory of the wanted poster. In seventeenth- and eighteenth-century America, live and textual outlaw displays featured the body of the condemned and reflected the spectator's proximity to the scaffold. Execution was a live, collaborative, and extremely popular religious performance in colonial America. Puritan ministers framed the condemned's public appearance and execution in terms of the Christian narrative of sin and redemption and displayed the prisoner as an example of the lessons offered in their sermons. The grim woodcuts featured on execution broadsides visualized not only the hanged corpse but also the crowd gathered to witness the outlaw's final punishment. The requisite humility before God exercised in Puritan religious communities required an empathic mode of spectatorship from members of the crowd: There but for the grace of God go I.

By the early part of the eighteenth century, printers and lawyers had replaced ministers to become the dominant cultural mediators of crime and punishment. As a result, representations of crime and punishment began to include more worldly concerns. Increasingly, printers and court reporters narrated the outlaw's life according to the norms of the secular biography, case history, or trial report. In terms of the imagery reproduced on execution broadsides, this narrative development was reflected through a shift in visual attention from the stage of punishment to the scene of the crime. These historical changes in the practice of outlaw display produced a new mode of spectatorship. In early nineteenth-century crime broadsides, information and arousal trumped older, more empathic ways of seeing crime and punishment. Dwight Conquergood describes this development as a shift from one structure of feeling to another: from the Puritan structure of feeling to the gothic sensibility (351). The gothic view of criminals, as moral monsters who ought to be repudiated (expelled) through practices of visual consumption (incorporation), signals the beginning of the age of America's moralistic consumer culture and moves us one step closer to the vigilante viewer.

The rise of the wanted poster tracks the shift from live outlaw displays to fugitive outlaw displays, or from a set of popular representational practices trained on the already captured body of the condemned man or woman on the scaffold to vernacular and later professional police texts that describe and picture missing bodies that need to be captured. Chapter 2 opens the history of fugitive display with the vernacular print cultures of colonial and antebellum America. The practice of posting "wanted," "stolen," or "missing" goods and services facilitated commerce and was a useful means of disciplining those who wished to participate in the market. Southern whites relied heavily on the surveillance function of print culture to control the slave population. Slave advertisements drew their power from an elaborate code of violent punishment. If the typical nature of woodcuts facilitated identification between spectators and the figure of the condemned in the Puritan imagination, in slave advertisements it reflected and facilitated the lack of nuance characteristic of racist practices of looking.

In the nineteenth century zoologists photographed slaves in the style of the anthropological mug shot as a means of proving their absolute otherness. Planters used photography to document their property. In the first practice slave portraits visualized racial typology: the individual slave served as a representative for the race. In the second case photography recorded the unique features of a particular slave and, thereby, served the purpose of identification. As mentioned previously, the earliest known photographic reward notice made and circulated in the United States is a homemade handbill for a fugitive slave. In this poster what had been two distinct traditions in American visual cultures of crime and punishment converge: punitive displays of condemned persons and instrumental notices advertising "wanted," "stolen," or "missing" property. In so far as it combines a makeshift mug shot with a physical description and call for capture, this text is an early approximation of the modern-day wanted poster.

Historians point to the American social reforms of the nineteenth century as the beginning of the end of public execution in the United States. However, the rise of lynching after the Civil War suggests that many whites held onto a tradition of spectacular torture featuring the black body. The late nineteenth century was a time of zealous recommitment to the gore and brutality of the public execution among white Southern evangelical Protestants. The terrorizing effects of lynching were extended through whites' practices of documenting and mass-reproducing the scenes of torture. Carried or mailed far from the scene of punishment, lynching postcards paradoxically reinforced the primitive function of group violence through modern networks of communication and individual acts of consumption. In sharp contrast to Puritan religious frames, which encouraged observers at an execution to practice empathic ways of seeing, Southern evangelical Protestant frames elicited violent participation and pornographic practices of looking.

Chapter 3 narrates the adoption of vernacular practices of outlaw display by professional detectives. Over the latter half of the nineteenth century, as violence became the exclusive provenance of the professional police in the North, official outlaw displays curated by urban detectives became charged interfaces between the police and the public and, therefore, prime sites for the negotiation of police power. During this era rogues' galleries displayed in city police departments were immensely popular attractions, which offered viewers an opportunity to be seen contemplating outlaw images in public. Displaying sets of outlaws, all in a row, the rogues' gallery cultivated a touristic gaze in visitors to the police station or detective's office. In these early displays photography served as visual proof of the popular belief that criminals constituted a biologically distinct and inferior class of persons. The rogues' galleries that sprang up all over the country were so popular that the police soon had to set limits on the public's access to fugitive displays.

As the owner of the largest collection of criminal portraits in the United States and founder of the first national detective agency, Allan Pinkerton professionalized the work of detection, in part, by limiting public access to his collection of criminal portraits. In the absence of a federal police force, Pinkerton's National Detective Agency played a prominent role in law enforcement throughout the United States during the latter half of the nineteenth century. As a result Pinkerton's found itself beholden to the public, even though, for the most part, the private agency did not earn its keep by them. Pinkerton worked public relations on two fronts, negotiating the growing tension between sober and romantic depictions of the work of detection. Sober images won the detectives distinction from the money-grubbing work of the bounty hunter, but they carried the unpopular threat of police surveillance over ordinary citizens.

Near the end of the century, as the agency came under fire for its antilabor practices, Pinkerton's sons turned decisively toward romantic depictions of the agency's work. They appropriated an amateur painting of a Western bandit, displayed the image prominently in their offices, and reproduced it on their publicity materials for years to come. Pinkerton's practices of outlaw display were intended to reassure viewers that the police were after hardened criminals, not criminalized populations of ordinary Americans, such as workers on strike. Significantly, romantic uses of the outlaw shifted the location of vigilante violence in the American imaginary from the American South to the Wild West, thereby disavowing the historical articulation between American outlaw displays and race-based surveillance practices.

Chapter 4 tracks the Federal Bureau of Investigation's practices of fugitive display. In the early part of the twentieth century, the FBI stressed the wanted poster's performance of emergency in order to communicate the necessity of intensive and extensive federal surveillance. In the World War I–era wanted poster for Grover Bergdoll, two print genres converge: war propaganda and tabloid journalism. The key to their convergence lies with Bergdoll's status as the "number-one" or "most wanted" enemy of the United States. It demonstrates the federal government's power to observe, rank, and file its citizens in times of war. And it foreshadows the rather bizarre cultural practice of ordering and displaying outlaws hierarchically that would become increasingly popular with the American public over the first half of the twentieth century. As a result, the text's address oscillates between being pedagogical, like the execution sermon (i.e., making an example of the outlaw), and being voyeuristic, like the rogues' gallery (i.e., making a curiosity of the outlaw). Because he's number one, Grover Bergdoll's outlaw appearance is at once more serious and more stimulating.

In the interwar years crime was treated as an exaggerated version of the lax morals thought to be sweeping the nation via the new pleasures available through the mass media and rampant practices of consumption. Popular moral panics expressed in these terms created an environment ripe for J. Edgar Hoover's masculine takeover of the FBI and the expansion of domestic surveillance. Increasingly sophisticated methods of data collection and filtering produced a new mode of display, whose drama derived from the filtering of the individual from the crowd—a technique that captured the popular imagination during an era characterized by the rapid growth of mass culture and attendant cultural fears regarding homogenization and anonymity. The "public enemy" served as a proxy for working through moral panics regarding the degeneration of the American character in a consumer society. By midcentury Hoover was using the "most wanted" outlaws to promote the Bureau's authority and deflect the American public's attention away from the fact that it was increasingly under surveillance. The program encouraged routine consumption of spectacular outlaw displays, while the Bureau's *Uniform Crime Reports* habituated the vigilante viewer to the temporality of crime waves and popularized the notion that violent crime was consistently on the rise.

Chapter 5 addresses the emergence of the interactive television program *America's Most Wanted* in the late 1980s. In the semantic shift from the "FBI's" to "America's" most wanted, the home viewer was promoted to the status of "partner" to the police. The program assumed a supportive and celebratory attitude toward police work. *America's Most Wanted* emerged in the context of the effective dismantling of the welfare state and the rise of the law-and-order approach to social problems in the 1980s and 1990s. The program answered to popular fantasies for a return to community policing. *America's Most Wanted* differed from police displays insofar as it cultivated categorical involvement in crime fighting from viewers, not just those who might recognize the fugitive or circumstance presented.

America's Most Wanted signaled the privatization of fugitive display—its entrance into the home. The privatization of fugitive display was a product not only of the wanted poster's migration to the medium of television. *America's Most Wanted* couched crime and punishment within a therapeutic discourse, where the punishment of criminals became "the first step toward healing" for the victims of violent crime. The address employed was no longer exclusively the sober technocratic address of a J. Edgar Hoover, but the split address of John Walsh, who was sometimes a sober expert and at other times an outraged member of the victims' rights movement. As a prominent member of the conservative movement and founder of the National Center for Missing and Exploited Children, Walsh helped

to bring the missing child to prominence as an ideological figure of innocence in the American popular imagination. Over the course of the show's
run, it increasingly split airtime between fugitive and victim displays. The
program juxtaposed displays of guilt and innocence through the twin televisual frames of the wanted poster and the missing notice. The vigilante
viewer's habit of consuming outlaw and victim displays in tandem, as
it were, prepped her for the federal government's framing of the events
of 9/11.

The conclusion closes the history of fugitive display with a discussion of
displays of the missing and wanted in the "war on terror." In the immediate
aftermath of the terrorist attacks of September 11, 2001, some New Yorkers
papered the city walls with missing posters for their lost loved ones. Vernacular texts, the missing fliers were tools of recovery and eventually became public memorials to individual victims. The missing-person flyers
addressed readers and listeners as insiders or members of a moral community of suffering and shared trauma. This address inadvertently referenced
the conservative embrace of the victim in the 1980s and 1990s, in whose
name calls were made for greater police power and harsher sentencing. In
effect, many Americans had been conditioned by the victim and outlaw
displays of the 1980s and 1990s to respond to vernacular displays of the
missing with naive moral outrage.

When President George W. Bush called for the capture of Osama bin
Laden, "Dead or Alive," he placed the villain squarely within the iconic
wanted poster of the Wild West. The president's "cowboy rhetoric" articulated the perceived boundary violation of the terrorist attacks to the American myth of innocence lost, which left the events of 9/11 ripe for cooptation
by gendered and racist ideologies and the iconography of the frontier
imaginary. Swept up in the cultural narrative of innocence lost and the
iconography of vigilante justice, the missing-person flyers became signs of
national innocence. In the 9/11 missing posters the lost innocence of the
missing individual became the lost childhood of the nation. Thus, vernacular and presidential practices of "facing" the events of 9/11 installed a new
field of social relations between people and images in which the missing
and the wanted functioned as intermediaries and scapegoats for American
readers, many of whom were fast becoming vigilante viewers for the "war
on terror."

The history of fugitive display is, by definition, a story about what the authorities lack. The cultivation of an audience of vigilante viewers, who are sympathetic to what the authorities want without experiencing that lack as a weakness, is a remarkable political achievement. It did not happen overnight. Nor was it a smooth, linear progression from the slave hunter to the imagined interactivity of the law-and-order citizen. Cultivated in fits and starts, the vigilante viewer is a product of individual decisions, vernacular traditions, institutional imperatives, signal events, public pressures, and the contradictions of consumer culture and the national imaginary. And yet, despite the messy and highly contingent history of outlaw display and consumption required to make the vigilante viewer, definite patterns emerge. As the histories gathered here reveal, Americans have yet to adequately examine some of the more distinctive—and, one could argue, sinister—aspects of their visual cultures of crime and punishment.

CHAPTER ONE

Execution Broadsides

THE CULTURAL PRACTICE OF MAKING AN EXAMPLE OF the outlaw can be traced back to the American literary genre of the execution sermon. Execution was a live, collaborative, and extremely popular religious performance in colonial America.[1] The broadly participatory nature of execution reflected its ritual function within Puritan religious communities. The communication rituals that surrounded the scaffold rehearsed the Christian narrative of sin and redemption while celebrating the spectacle of the punishable body. Puritan ministers presided over executions and "displayed the prisoner as a 'sorrowful spectacle' and embodied 'example,' a focal point and prop for the minister's fiery execution sermon" (Conquergood 345). Ministers made an example of the criminal and used his poignant embodiment of sin to harness the crowd's excitement for God's work. This was no easy task, because the collective energy of the crowd was likely inspired by the event but also overlaid with the drama of personal relationships and the lusty possibilities inherent in the act of crowding together. Ministers tried to discipline the lust out of crowds by holding the fate of the condemned's soul (and by proxy their own) over their heads.

Framed in spiritual terms by Puritan ministers, the condemned man or woman was not so different from the onlookers gathered to watch him be put to death. As the minister reminded them, sin moved through the religious community and could worm its way into the heart of any man, woman, or child. The requisite humility before God exercised in Puritan religious communities required an empathic mode of spectatorship from members of the crowd: There but for the grace of God go I. "This way of seeing," writes Dwight Conquergood, "encouraged a deeply sympathetic, theatrical identification in which the spectators could imaginatively exchange places with the condemned, instead of holding themselves aloof in distanced judgment. The ideal spectator at executions became a deeply engaged co-performative witness" (351).

Crime and Punishment Literature

According to historian Daniel A. Cohen, execution sermons were delivered on the Sunday before or the day of the execution, then printed and sold as soon as possible after the execution, usually within two weeks if possible. Execution sermons were most likely sold directly to readers from a printer's shop or bookseller and/or distributed in rural areas by chapmen, who traveled the countryside selling wares. Cohen notes that execution sermons, which were published as pamphlets, were extremely cheap and would have been affordable to "all but the poorest of New England readers." Distribution was widespread. He estimates that there was one execution sermon for every two Boston households and notes that a single pamphlet probably circulated among many readers. The publication of other types of sermons often relied upon public or private financing, but execution sermons more than paid for themselves (4–6).

Other types of crime writing were sometimes appended to execution sermons, including confessions and warnings delivered by the condemned, dialogues between ministers and condemned criminals, and factual accounts.[2] Among the types of crime literature sold with execution sermons, the last- or dying-words genre, imported from England and Scotland, was by far the most popular. Because of the condemned's unique position on the threshold between life and death, his or her words were thought to possess wisdom not otherwise accessible to the reader (Cohen 7–10). The dramatic power of such speeches, writes Conquergood, lay in the condemned's proximity to death: "The 'last Dying Words' of the condemned gathered compelling presencing powers precisely because they were uttered from a space of death and disappearance that impressed on the audience the urgency of their vanishing" (345).

While the execution sermon was an invention of Puritan New England, the genre of "last or dying words" can be traced back to the tradition of the scaffold speech in England. Political prisoners delivered the earliest scaffold speeches. Later, common criminals shared dying words. The earliest "last-words" ballad in the collection at the National Library of Scotland dates to 1700 and includes a woodcut featuring one man vaguely pointing his bow and arrow at a second man.[3] The ballad is entitled "The Last Words of James Mackpherson, Murderer." It begins:

> I spent my time in rioting,
> debauch'd my health and strength,
> I pillag'd, plundered, murdered,
> but now alas! at length,
> I'm brought to punishment condign,
> pale Death draws near to me,
> The end I ever did project
> to hang upon a Tree.

According to the library, although Mackpherson was guilty of some of the crimes of which he was accused, political intrigue sealed his fate. Legend has it that Mackpherson performed his last-words poem on the scaffold for the crowd gathered to watch him hang. He then took out his fiddle and played an original tune. After finishing the song, he offered the instrument to the crowd. No one came forward to claim the fiddle. Like the first rock star, Mackpherson smashed his fiddle and was executed.[4]

Despite the literary conceit that condemned prisoners delivered these speeches from the scaffold and on the brink of death, they were often prepared in advance of the public execution and reflected the combined efforts of criminals, printers, ministers, and jail officers, who compiled a compelling narrative during the days leading up to an execution (Cohen 20). The collaborative, or perhaps even compulsory, aspect of last and dying verses is borne out by the fact that they retained the pedagogical function and tone of the execution sermon well into the eighteenth century. Although the voice is now purportedly the criminal's instead of the minister's, the condemned presents his self to the crowd as an example of what will happen if those listening to or reading his words stray from God. Consider, for example, the opening lines from an execution broadside published in Boston in 1738, entitled *The Dying Lamentation and Advice of Philip Kennison:*

> Good People all both great and small,
> to whom these Lines should come,
> A warning take by my sad Fall,
> and unto God return.

A few lines later Kennison makes a special appeal to the young:

> Oh let me then this Caution give,
> to every one of you,
> Especially to you that live,
> in Sin and spend your Youth.

The journalistic quality of dying verses, by comparison to execution sermons, is attributable not only to the shift from the minister's to the criminal's voice but also to their unique temporality on the threshold between life and death. The Kennison execution broadside features a woodcut of a winged figure of death holding a reaper in one hand and an hourglass in the other. The illustration is labeled "TIME." A line guaranteeing the authorship of the broadside further underscores its liminal status: "All written in his own Hand, a few Days before his Death." Proximity to death lends Kennison's words an air of spiritual enlightenment, but it would come to signify earthly authenticity as execution broadsides became increasingly secular in tone and content over the course of the eighteenth century.

Execution broadsides offered more factual information about the criminal and his deeds than execution sermons or dying verses had. *The Last Speech and Dying Advice of Poor Julian,* printed in Boston in 1733, offers a rich example from this transitional period in the history of crime literature. The author narrates his servant's upbringing, refers to the particular crime with which he has been charged, and pleads innocence. Even so, he ultimately capitulates to the Christian frame of sin and redemption and repents: "Whereas I have been charged with and tried for burning my Master's barn, I now declare as a dying man that I did not do it, nor was I in any way privy to it." After a paragraph break Julian goes on to contradict his plea of innocence: "I acknowledge that I deserve to die, and would confess especially my Drunkenness and Sabbath-breaking, which have led me to this great Sin for which I now must die." The text's internal contradictions suggest that it was the product of a "collaborative" writing process, caught somewhere between secular biography and moral pedagogy.

The elaborate woodcut featured on the execution broadside for "Poor Julian" appends portraits of the criminal to the scaffold scene. In this manner the image reflects the growing attention being paid to the biographical details of criminals' lives. On the right-hand side the image depicts four figures, including Julian and possibly his master (as indicated by the fancy dress) or perhaps a typical image of drunkenness (given the belly on the figure and his off-kilter posture). The other figures are difficult to make out. The left side of the image depicts action. The setting is established by a windmill structure that may represent the barn Julian was accused of burning. Julian ascends the ladder to the scaffold at gunpoint. Dwarfed by these images is a scaffold scene. Julian stands in a cart on wheels. There is a rope around his neck, which is fastened to the scaffold. He is waiting to die. The image is not perspectival, or rather, it appears to employ several perspectives at once. This may be the effect of combining panels from several different woodcuts. In the resultant image the size of the figures does not necessarily represent their distance from the viewer or their spatial relationships to one another; however, the biographical portraits of Julian (and possibly his master) are considerably larger than the scaffold scene.

The entire panel is overlaid and captioned with bible verses, which depict salvation as a physical process of being washed clean by God: "Deliver me from Blood-Guiltiness, O God, thou God of my Salvation: and my Tongue shall sing aloud of thy Righteousness"; "Come now let us Reason together, Sayeth the Lord: though your sins be as scarlet, they shall be as white as snow: though they be red like crimson, they shall be as wool." In the relationship between word and image, one can see the growing tension between ritualistic and documentary methods of depicting crime and punishment in the eighteenth century.

By the end of the century, information about the crimes committed and

Pfal. LI. 14. *Deliver me from Blood-Guiltiness, O God, thou God of my Salvation: and my Tongue shall sing aloud of thy Righteousness.* Isa. I. 18. *Come now and let us Reason together, saith the Lord: though your sins be as scarlet, they shall be as white as snow: though they be red like crimson, they shall be as wool.*

The last SPEECH and dying ADVICE of

poor' Julian,

Who was Executed the 22d of *March*, 1733. for the Murder of Mr. *John Rogers* of *Pembroke*. Written with his own Hand, and delivered to the Publisher the Day before his Execution.

FRom my Childhood to Twenty Years of Age, I liv'd in a Family where I was learnt to Read and say my Catechism, and had a great deal of Pains taken with me.—— And in my younger Years I was under some Convictions and Awakenings, and concern'd about the Condition of my Soul ;—— and I had many Warnings in the Providence of God to turn from my Sins—— But I have (and I desire to lament it) abused God's Patience and Goodness to me, and apostatised from God and good Beginnings, and now I have forsaken God, he has forsaken me, and I acknowledge he has been just in leaving me, so that I have gone from bad to worse, till for my Sins I am now to die.

Whereas I have been charged with and tried for burning my Master's Barn, I now declare as a dying Man that I did not do it, nor was I any way privy to it.

I acknowledge I deserve to die, and would confess especially my Drunkenness and Sabbath-breaking, which have led me to this great Sin for which I now die.

I desire therefore that all, and especially Servants, would take Warning by me ; I am a dying Man, just going to leave this World, and the Thoughts of it terrify me, knowing how unfit I am to appear before my Judge.

O beware of sinning as I have done—— Beware of Drunkenness, of Sabbath-breaking, and of running away from your Masters, and don't put away the Thoughts of Death and of Judgment: I once put these Things far away, but now they are near, and I am going to appear before my great and terrible Judge, which surprizeth me beyond what I am able to express.

If you have been instructed and catechized from your Childhood, and joined your selves to Assemblies in which the Lord Jesus Christ is most purely worshipped, then let me warn and charge you to beware of casting off the Things that are good, lest God leave you to your selves, and you go on in Sin till you come to the greatest Wickedness.

O take Warning by me all of you, I intreat you—— See and fear and do no more so wickedly as I have done.

O let me once more intreat you all, especially Servants, to beware of the Sin of Drunkenness, and be obedient to your Masters ; don't run away from them, nor get Drunk, for if you do it will bring you to Ruine as it has done me.

I call to you now as one come from the Dead, to turn from your evil Ways while you have Time, and not put off your Repentance to another Day, lest you then call and God will not answer you.

My Master often told me that my Sins would bring me to this, but I little thought that it would be so.

I return my hearty Thanks to the Rev. Ministers who have taken Pains to assist me in preparing for my latter End. And as I desire to be forgiven, so I forgive all Mankind.

These Things I declare freely and voluntarily, and desire Mr. *Fleet* to Print the same for the Benefit of the Living : And I do hereby utterly disown and disclaim all other Speeches, Papers or Declarations that may be printed in my Name, as Witness my Hand this 21st. of *March*, 1733.

Julian.

Witness
Zach. Trescott.

Printed and Sold by T. Fleet, at the Heart and Crown in Cornhill, Boston.

The Last Speech and Dying Advice of Poor Julian, Boston, 1733.
(Courtesy American Antiquarian Society)

details of the criminal's biography took precedence over moral lessons drawn from a particular set of crimes and their punishment. Cohen argues that these developments in the print culture of crime and punishment are attributable to the changing landscape of New England. In the early decades of the century, New England became more diverse in terms of religious practice and more contested in terms of political beliefs.[5] At the same time printers and booksellers multiplied and grew more aggressive in their attempts to market literature to an expanding reading public. By the 1730s printers and lawyers had replaced ministers as the cultural mediators of crime and punishment. As a result, representations of crime and punishment became increasingly secular in tone (Cohen 23).

The Look of Death

As the text of execution broadsides became less formulaic, the woodcuts used to illustrate execution began to depict the practice as an earthly event that nevertheless bore traces of the minister's spiritual frame. The primitive woodcuts reproduced on execution broadsides featured the architecture of the scaffold, the dangling figure of the condemned, and the crowd gathered to witness the final punishment. God was present in the scaffold scenes reproduced on execution broadsides to the extent that the scene was rendered from on high and often included the framing convention of heavenly clouds. The all-seeing eye looked down on the crowd and the condemned. Grim woodcuts depicted the scene in somber and dramatic tones. The typical nature of these images suited the Christian narrative formula of sin and redemption. Scaffold illustrations were "to the point and not without emotive force. In the starkness of their style and the finality of their content, stock images of the gallows must have aroused at least a small *frisson* of pleasurable dread in many viewers" (Anderson 23).

While the woodcut is often described as a crude technology, its visual power lay precisely in its ability to render stark contrasts. In scaffold scenes the tension between life and death is communicated through the visual contrast of light and dark space. The woodcut featured on a 1795 broadside entitled *Dying Confession of Pomp, a Negro Man,* is exemplary. This image is typical in the sense that it resembles other woodcuts of scaffold scenes but also because this same woodcut would have been used over and over

Dying Confession of Pomp, a Negro Man, Boston, 1795.
(American Antiquarian Society)

again to illustrate the executions of many different criminals: "The most far-sighted printers kept in stock sets of woodcuts showing various numbers of criminals being hanged" (Collison 34). While the text of the broadside repeatedly marks Pomp's race and status as a servant, the illustration pictures him like any other man condemned to death.

In the woodcut featured on *Dying Confession of Pomp,* one's eye is first drawn to the hanging man on the scaffold. The condemned is spotlighted by the use of white space around his figure, but the scaffold is the most prominent element of the image. Spatially, it serves to connect heaven and earth. It appears as though the ladder that leads the prisoner up the scaffold also directs him to heaven. Remarkably, the hanging figure dangles above the crowd gathered to watch him be put to death, as if to signify his spiritual ascent. The inclusion of the crowd in the scaffold scene reminds present-day readers of the relay of gazes at work in the visual culture of a live execution. In this woodcut members of the crowd are pictured with raised sticks or guns, which signify their violent condemnation of the criminal. This crowd appears more lusty than sympathetic. The props held by the onlookers suggest that members of the crowd actively participated in transporting the condemned from the prison to the scaffold.

Reports of Crime and Punishment

In the late eighteenth and early nineteenth centuries, crime reports vied with execution broadsides in terms of their popularity. Crime reports reflected little to no trace of the minister's authority. In fact, some early crime reports engage in the regional practice of sharing stories about the dreadful things that happen to other people in one's community. The storied surveillance of crime reports circulated for a local audience is closely related to gossip, implying not only highly localized practices of spying but also accompanying acts of judgment.

Consider, for example, an early American crime broadside published in 1801, entitled "Horrid Murder and Suicide," which features a woodcut of a row of coffins at the top. The case described is that of a woman murdering some of her children and then killing herself. To reflect this, four coffins represent the number of the dead, growing gradually smaller as the eye moves across the page from left to right, indicating that the first coffin is hers and the rest are for her children, arranged in order of age and size. The broadside is subtitled, "A Narrative of one of the most Shocking and Tragical Catastrophes, that ever blackened the Catalogue of human events, which happened the 6th September, 1801, at a place called Paliz 14 miles from Poughkeepsie, State of New-York." This broadside is a clear precursor to the tabloids, but with a difference: while this is sensationalist literature, there is yet a real sense of local concern and interest. At the bottom of the broadside are two footnotes in italics: *"*What a remarkable number of melancholy events have taken place in this country, within the space of a few months! How many have been registered among the dead, by Suicides, Murders and by Duels. Alas, what deprav'd creatures we are! / She very deliberately call'd a chill to have its hair comb'd and then cut its throat."* Here, the sensational narrative is followed by a quick reflection on what this means about "our" community, about humanity, and then by a final return to the most astonishing detail of the case.

By the early nineteenth century journalistic techniques for narrating and picturing crime and punishment dominated. The condemned was no longer primarily understood in terms of a spiritual biography, authored by a minister, for whom he or she embodied a particular passage of scripture, or a bit of local news passed on by a neighbor, for whom the condemned represented a rift in the fabric of life. Increasingly, printers and court reporters narrated the outlaw's life according to the norms of the secular biography, case history, or trial report. Concurrently, the focus of outlaw displays shifted from the execution scene to the murder scene and from the generic figure of the dangling corpse to criminal portraiture.

A lengthy broadside entitled *The Awful Beacon to the Rising Generation,* printed in Boston in 1821, includes not one but three illustrations: the murder scene, the murderer in prison, and the scaffold scene. The broadside employs a broad public address. Its rhetoric and tone are secular:

> WE here present the public with a view of the wretched POWERS, in the act of murdering the unfortunate and unsuspecting Victim of his Revenge—who, from concurring circumstances, it is probable he decoyed to his house under the pretence of FRIENDSHIP, that he might there commit that "deed of dreadful note" which he had long premeditated, and for which he has been so justly condemned to suffer! With repeated declarations that malice on his part was no longer harboured, and with assurances of friendship, the innocent KENNEDY was induced too hastily to credit the monster's vile pretensions of reconciliation!

The broadside's author, who displays Powers to the public, also claims membership in that public. Sensationalism becomes a form of heightened realism and a credit to the author's powers of observation and the writer's craft. The criminal no longer plays the role of condemned sinner. He has become a monster. The lesson offered to readers of the broadside is behavioral rather than moral: Beware of the wolf in sheep's clothing.

The moment of truth has shifted from God's judgment enacted on the scaffold to man's character revealed on earth. While God is mentioned in this broadside, he does not appear until the final word of the second full paragraph, coming into the picture as the one who helped the law to find Powers. The broadside recounts how a local townsperson spotted Powers and turned him in, but this decisive act is ultimately attributed to God. This element is a holdover from earlier broadsides where divine signs or magic events helped lead the authorities to the offending individual. But it also reflects the shift in popular interest from the scaffold to the manhunt. Here, God works through the lay detective or informant rather than the executioner.[6]

Significantly, the notice references the dwindling of pubic execution, now officiously framed as a legal practice:

> In the criminal code of the humane and intelligent State of Massachusetts, few offences are even now considered so utterly desperate as to justify the awful award of a public and violent death from the hands of man. But odious Murder, of the first degree, in ATROCIOUS MALICE, receives as it ought, the Death of the Cord. The wretched Powers has been sentenced to die ignominiously—not only as a just punishment for the horrid crime of which he has been convicted, but as an example to all others, of the vengeance which always pursues the steps of the Murderer, whom no art can save from the sword of justice in this life; and whose only hope in the world to come must depend on the mercies of the Almighty.

Public execution has become a deterrent to crime. The law will teach the murderer, and by extension the reader, a lesson. Powers serves as an example of the law's power to punish, rather than as an embodiment of sin, and God is obliquely referenced as a weak and fading last hope.

In the illustrations featured on this broadside, it is possible to see the rising importance of the murder scene and the dwindling significance of the execution scene. The relative positioning and space allotted to each image reflect a shift in the reader's priorities. Murder has clearly become the broadside's selling point. The view represented in the first two images is man-to-man rather than God's view on the action. The murder scene is six times the size of the prison scene, which is approximately double the size of the scaffold scene. In this broadside the scaffold image moves down the page, from the prominent headline position to a miniaturized endnote. It is so small compared to the other illustrations that it looks like a stamp or seal, rather than an illustration of the text. Indeed, this last image does not so much illustrate the narrative as mark its conclusion.

There is another important factor in the diminishment of the scaffold scene. The popularization of wood engraving, together with early nineteenth-century advances in mechanized printing, made illustration increasingly available to a widening public (Anderson 18). Since the wood-engraving technique itself allowed for greater precision, wood engravings mark a shift from the generic figure of the condemned or a block print of a

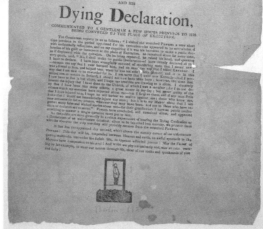

The Awful Beacon to the Rising Generation, Boston, ca. 1821. (Courtesy Rare Book and Special Collections Division, Library of Congress)

coffin to mock-realist portraits of particular individuals to be hanged. I say "mock realist" because these images, although more specific and concrete in the visual detail they offered, were reused over and over again and so did not necessarily bear a resemblance to the particular individual storied on a given broadside (Collison 39).

The Awful Beacon presages the photographic wanted poster of the late nineteenth century insofar as a desire for the mug shot is reflected in the generic prisoner's portrait. The visual transition from woodcuts of hanging corpses seen from a great distance to frontal and profile wood engravings of individual prisoners reflects the translation of the condemned into the criminal over the course of nineteenth century. If the condemned was a synecdoche for the evil that circulated throughout the community, the criminal was a discrete figure who could be separated out from the rest of society. And as punishment becomes a secular matter overseen by professionals, condemnation and forgiveness are no longer necessarily interconnected ways of seeing crime and punishment.

American Gothic

These historical changes in the practice of outlaw display produced a new mode of spectatorship. In early nineteenth-century crime broadsides, information and arousal trumped older, more empathic ways of seeing crime and punishment. Dwight Conquergood describes this development as a shift from one structure of feeling to another: "The Puritan structure of feeling that embraced wrongdoers as members of the same moral community in need of repentance was superceded in the nineteenth century by a gothic view of criminals as 'moral aliens' and 'moral monsters'" (351). The gothic view of criminals as moral others, who ought to be repudiated (expelled) through practices of visual consumption (incorporation), signals the beginning of the age of America's moralistic consumer culture and moves us one step closer to the vigilante viewer.

The shift in visual attention from the scaffold to the murder scene brought about a corresponding fascination with the victims of violent crimes. A broadside entitled *Lines in Commemoration of the Death of Sarah M. Cornell* is exemplary of the importance of the victim in gothic crime literature. The broadside features striking woodcuts of Sarah M.

Cornell, hanged by a deceitful reverend, who seduced her with his "artful tongue." Murder stories had truth-value not so much because they were factual, but because they offered a moral, and increasingly behavioral, lesson to the reader. The verse ends with a melancholy warning to all young women in its purview:

> Ye maids around in virgin bloom,
>   With youth art beauty blessed;
> Beware the crime for fear the doom,
>   Of *Sarah* pierce your breast.

This particular broadside is historically significant as a transitional text not only because it marks the shift from Puritanical empathy to gothic sensationalism but also because the condemned murderer is a minister. The broadside features two poems and two grisly woodcuts of the murdered woman: in one she is pictured as she was found, hung by her murderer; the second woodcut is of a coffin bearing her initials. The broadside adds a morbid flourish: a braided rope forms the border that divides one poem from the other. The first poem is a classic folk ballad of seduction and murder, while the second closely resembles crime reporting, giving information regarding the reverend's trial and escape and the reward offer of three hundred dollars for his capture.

The remainder of the second poem, attributed to the victim, begins, "Me thought I heard her spirit say." Sarah then issues a warning to maidens both old and young, asks her friends not to be sad at their loss, and says goodbye. The final stanza reads:

> Yet to conclude this mournful song
> These lines I pray remember long:
> Adieu! My friends, pray don't repine,
> Examples yours, experience mine.

In this last line the poet recognizes the border that divides the experience of violence from the burden of serving as an exemplar. In this nineteenth-century broadside death makes Sarah into an example, a lesson, and a warning to others, who are encouraged to identify with the victim of violent crime instead of the perpetrator. Significantly, the shift in attention from the condemned to his victim signals a corresponding change in the function of

Lines in Commemoration of the Death of Sarah M. Cornell, Philadelphia, 1833. (Courtesy Rare Book and Special Collections Division, Library of Congress)

these figures. Sarah does not exemplify sin and redemption, because she did nothing wrong. Or rather, her mistake is framed in secular terms as a lack of judgment: trusting the minister's station in life, she misjudged his character. In other words, what we have here is a class drama: the sensational story of a fallen clergyman and an unsuspecting virgin, who did not sufficiently guard her chastity.

The secularization of crime literature influenced how people regarded one another and shaped their attitudes toward punishment in particular. The visual practice of reading the things and people of this earth as signs of divine will, as well as the specialized seeing of reading the body and behavior of the condemned for signs of the salvation or damnation of his or her immortal soul, was replaced by the practice of reading crime literature for evidence of one's own social standing. As morality became coded in class rather than religious terms, the spectacle of the condemned no longer signified the capacity for sin shared by all, but instead reflected the visible differences between the upstanding viewer and the morally decrepit and desperate criminal.

Advertisement for an Execution

Public execution was gradually abolished on a state-by-state basis over the course of the nineteenth and twentieth centuries. As American society became more secular, the air of providence surrounding public hangings dissipated. In its place ministers and concerned citizens delivered hand-wringing sermons that struggled with execution as something that had become a Christian burden. This turn of events was brought on by several related historical developments, including changes in Christian doctrine and the professionalization of medicine and police work. Historian Elizabeth Clark attributes decreased tolerance for spectacles of suffering to significant developments in religious and medical thought. For Clark the liberalization of Christian doctrine and the invention of anesthesia conspired to create a new, celebratory attitude toward the body.[7] Consequently, public spectacles of physical suffering took on new meaning.

Execution broadsides disappeared in America at the beginning of the nineteenth century (Cohen 25), but other types of printed ephemera attest to the continuation of the practice of public execution. Remaining evidence suggests that crowds continued to flock to public hangings and take pleasure in the spectacle of death so long as such events were held. Some executions were framed as excursions. The following notice, printed in Alton, Illinois, on June 12, 1841, advertises a steamboat trip to the site of the execution and back:

> NOTICE. The undersigned, having chartered the steamboat Eagle for the purpose of accommodating all the citizens of Alton and the vicinity, who may wish to see the MURDERERS HUNG at St. Louis, on the 9th day of July next, would inform the public that the Boat will leave this place at *Seven O'clock, A. M.,* and leave St. Louis at about *Four, P.M.,* so as to reach home the same evening. The Boat will be repaired and fitted up for the occasion; and every attention will be paid to the comfort of Passengers. *Fare for the Trip to St. Louis and back will be* $1 50. . . . A BAND OF MUSIC may be expected to accompany the Boat.

Framed as an excursion, the scaffold scene attains the status of entertainment without moralizing. Day-trippers have more need of the diversions offered by a band on a boat than the oversight of God. The execution becomes a tourist destination, which suggests its removal from the life of the community. It belongs to a separate space and time. The well-appointed ship serves as a metaphor for the removal of execution from the domain of tradition to the big city, where it becomes more purely a spectator's sport. Notably, one no longer purchases the broadside for its ritual, entertainment, or informational value. Instead, the broadside advertises the event to readers, who must pay to get closer to the action.

CHAPTER TWO

Slave Notices

THE HISTORY OF FUGITIVE, AS OPPOSED TO LIVE, outlaw displays can be traced to the vernacular print cultures of colonial and antebellum America. The practice of posting "wanted," "stolen," or "missing" goods and services facilitated commerce and was a useful means of disciplining those who wished to participate in the market. To "post" a man was to expose him through the public display of written testimony about his character (e.g., "I'll post you for a swindler and a coward," or "If you don't pay up, I'll post you for a defaulter").[1] As a vernacular practice posting provided a powerful deterrent to bad business insofar as a man's name and reputation were at stake in a local community where many readers knew him personally.[2]

John Randolph of Louisiana provides us with a rich example of the artful verbal sparring that went on between men through the practice of posting. In August of 1835 he offered a five-hundred-dollar reward for the capture of "a *bloated, pusillanimous* Scoundrel, named ALFRED CUMMING, (but who suffered himself introduced to the people of this country as *Colonel* Cumming,) within the jurisdiction of our law; in order that the several suits for a *Libel, Perjury and damages,* may be instituted against him."[3] In the broadside Randolph accuses Cumming of lying to him in order to collect a debt in full before it was due and of tarnishing Randolph's reputation "through the medium of a Placard."

If to post a man was to shame him, to post goods and services was to advertise them. Thus, the commercial potential of posting was exploited in conjunction with its power to discipline those who did not play by the rules. Posted broadsides solicited services, attracted potential buyers, created an audience for confrontations, made disputes a matter of public record, and leveraged local readers' sense of right and wrong against offenders. Posting hailed the bodies of those not initially involved in a disagreement to become the readers and serve as judges in the communal court of the town square or the coffeehouse.

Runaway Notices

The rhetoric of shame was an effective means of disciplining those with the status of personhood rather than property. Posting temporarily turned the spotlight on particular property-owning white men accused of having done wrong, while on every side of the post, women, servants, free men, and slaves were perpetually under surveillance. In the American South whites routinely used newspapers and handbills to monitor and control the slave population.[4] The desire of Southern planters for systematic surveillance required them to enlist the support of whites without wealth and/or slaves. Regular publication and posting of runaway and "pickup" notices called into being a network of interested onlookers beyond the borders of the plantation, linking one plantation to the next, the city to the country, all in the name of protecting the private property of wealthy white Southerners.

Planters and other white Southerners published three different types of slave notices: runaway notices, "for sale" ads, and "pickup" notices. Akin to "missing" advertisements, runaway notices announced property out of place, but they also drew attention to a unique offense, capable of being committed only by persons with the status of property. The figure of the runaway slave was treated like property come to life. He or she possessed the uncanny power to steal him- or herself away and thereby posed a unique threat to the slave owner and to the entire plantation economy. Slave notices were therefore understood as a subset of stolen-property notices.

The relationship between stolen property and runaway slaves is visualized in the proximity of two ads, stacked atop one another in the *Virginia Gazette:* a runaway slave notice and a notice regarding the subscriber's stolen horse. Down the left side of the column, a sight line connects a generic woodcut of a slave figure to a generic woodcut of a horse, creating a visual equivalency between these two prized forms of personal property.

As was the case with the woodcuts used to illustrate execution broadsides, the same runaway woodcut was used over and over again across publications and repeated multiple times within the same publication. The familiar stamp of the runaway marked each runaway notice out from the rest of the ads on the page. Like woodcuts of lost or stolen horses, the generic runaway figure was shown in profile. Remarkably, the runaway figure was depicted in motion, as if caught in the act of running away—always with one foot off of the ground. Some woodcuts showed the runaway looking back over his shoulder at his pursuers. Others offered full-length profiles of a purposeful and determined runaway, whose attention was focused not on the viewer, but on the distance to be covered before him.

The repetition of the same woodcuts played against the individualizing text of the ads. According to Daniel Meaders, "The typical runaway advertisement contained a terse description of the fugitive's name, sex, physical traits, personal traits, and other characteristics" (288). While the text of the ad served as an instrument of individualization, the repeated visual of the generic runaway figure suggested that slaves were an undifferentiated and threatening mass that might revolt if not properly disciplined. If the typical nature of the woodcuts on execution broadsides facilitated identification between spectators and the figure of the condemned in the Puritan imagination, in slave advertisements it reflected and facilitated the lack of nuance and dedifferentiation characteristic of racist practices of looking. In the nineteenth century runaway notices became sex-specific in visual as well as verbal content, and a typical image of the female fugitive joined the typical image of the male fugitive in the columns of local newspapers.

In addition to runaway notices, papers published two other types of advertisements that monitored the circulation and mobility of slaves, considered, respectively, as commodities and suspicious persons: for-sale ads and pickup notices. While runaway notices warned the locals of a menace, for-sale ads described slaves in glowing terms (Meaders 289). Pickup

Lithograph Used in Antebellum Deep South Newspaper
Advertisements for the Recovery of Runaway Slaves, 1850.
(Courtesy Center for Louisiana Studies Digital Archives)

notices worked in tandem with the regular patrol of Southern cities by
wardens seeking runaways. If free men and women were caught without
proof of their status, or slaves were caught moving about the city unaccom-
panied and without a pass from their master, they were locked up in
workhouses until they could prove their status if free, or until their masters
reclaimed them if not. Periodically, wardens published descriptions of the
slaves in their keeping. If an owner recognized a description of one of his
slaves in the paper, he would contact the warden and promise to pay a fee to
have the slave delivered back to him.

Slave advertisements drew their power from an elaborate code of violence cloaked as discipline.[5] "Negro laws" lent vigilantism a quasi-official status in the antebellum South. In the nineteenth century, as the North moved toward a modern criminal justice system, the South continued to maintain order through customary codes that gave all whites informal police power over all blacks. The informality of the code worked well because its flexibility made it possible to keep order without undermining the planters' prerogatives.[6] The Negro laws outlined the grounds for harsh punishment of slaves who ran away, as well as of those persons who provided assistance or shelter to runaways. The code doubled as an elaborate system of threats, setting out the punishments appropriate to particular violations in morbid detail.

While slave notices primarily functioned through written texts, it was not uncommon for these texts to be performed by zealous readers. In the slave narrative of Lunsford Lane, written by William Hawkins, the author reports that it was common for white men to lounge about the stores in Raleigh, North Carolina, where Lane lived, and read slave advertisements aloud, "especially when slaves were present, and for their benefit." Reinforcing Lane's claim, Hawkins adds, "it may seem strange that the Southern people would be so unwise as to read such notices to their slaves, and yet we have abundant proof from living witnesses of escaped slaves, that such is the fact." In Lane's narrative the irony of such performances of white power becomes clear: whites read slave advertisements aloud in order to taunt or terrorize slaves within earshot, but the practice provided ancillary benefits to slaves, reminding them that escape was possible.

Family Matters

Penned by plantation owners, runaway notices are at times openly melodramatic, reverberating with the desires, dependencies, and denials characteristic of the slave economy. The emotional tone of some of these notices reveals the blurring of home and workplace that was a fact of life on plantations. Runaway notices staged events taking place in the relatively private space of the plantation for public consumption. Often, they did so without editing or even tempering the planter's emotional reaction to the event. This lack of self-consciousness on the part of planters reflected their unquestioned position of privilege within the social system.

Consider an 1863 handbill for a runaway slave named Dolly, crafted by a Southern planter named Louis Manigault.[7] The notice follows the conventions established in slave advertisements published in Southern newspapers since the colonial period—except, that is, for the inclusion of the fugitive's photograph. At a time when it was technologically impossible to reproduce photographs on a printing press, Manigault and the Augusta police literally cut out this woman's photograph and pasted it to a piece of paper torn from one of Manigault's plantation ledgers.[8] Directly above the fugitive's image, the poster announces a *"$50.00 Reward!!"* for her capture. Below her picture a lengthy paragraph, written out in longhand, describes her escape, her physical appearance and social manner, and her relationship to Louis Manigault—her owner and the author of the notice. The poster also contains contact information. Should someone spot the fugitive, they were to notify Antoine Poullain Esq. at the Augusta Police Station.

The runaway notice for Dolly highlights the caste and gender dimensions of status relationships in the plantation South.[9] According to Manigault's description of her, Dolly is both a missing family member and a wanted fugitive. The language that Manigault employs naturalizes his family's ownership of Dolly and at the same time suggests that her *belonging* extends beyond mere property relations. Dolly, he writes, "never changed her Owner and has been a house Servant always." Dolly's age and light complexion raise the question of whether or not she was, in fact, a family member—the offspring of Louis's father, Charles Manigault.

Manigault begins the notice by granting Dolly the agency and will to run away, but as his description unfolds, it becomes a rationalization for her disappearance. Dolly's status teeters between innocence and experience as the cause of her disappearance slips between "has been enticed off" and "ran away." Manigault effectively writes her out of the position of active agent and into the position of naive, passive victim: "It is thought," Manigault writes in a tone that obscures the thinker, "she has been enticed off by some White Man, being herself a Stranger to this City, and belonging to a Charleston family." In these few, short lines, Manigault places the responsibility for Dolly's disappearance with someone other than Dolly or himself

When Received.	Coveyance.	No. of bush. Rough Rice.	No. of bbls. Clean Rice.	No. of bus. to the bbl.	Prices.	Date of Sales.	Gross Amount of Sales.	Nett Amount of Sales.

$ 50.00 Reward !!

Ran away from the Yard Corner of Jackson & Broad Streets, Augusta Ga. — on the evening of Tuesday 7th April 1863 a Woman "Dolly", whose likeness is here seen. — She is thirty years of age, light complexion — hesitates somewhat when spoken to, and is not a very healthy woman — but rather good looking, with a fine set of teeth. Never changed her Owner and has been a house Servant always. — It is thought she has been enticed off by some White Man, being herself a Stranger to this City, and belonging to a Charleston family. — For further particulars apply to Antoine Poullain Esqr Augusta Ga. — "

Augusta Police Station

Louis Manigault, Owner of Dolly

Runaway Notice for Dolly, 1863. (Courtesy, Southern Historical Collection, Wilson Library, The University of North Carolina at Chapel Hill) and positions her as "belonging" to a Charleston family in the doubly interpretable sense of being a member of the family and being its possession. By naming Dolly a stranger to Augusta, Manigault subtly indicates that Dolly's disappearance is not her fault, but the fault of the Yankees who violently disrupted what he took to be the former tranquility of the Southern family.

While Manigault begins his poster with the announcement that Dolly has run away, clearly, he works against this explanation for her disappearance. As the text progresses, Manigault infantilizes Dolly so that he may secure her innocence and disavow the possibility that she would want to leave him or his family. He transforms a narrative of abandonment into a sensational story of kidnapping.[10] He triangulates his desire and disappointment, creating a third character in the drama. Projecting a villain responsible for his loss, Manigault creates distance between himself and this anonymous other: "some White Man." Again, the specter of the Yankee looms large behind this conspicuous and awkward marker. With this phrase Manigault indicts the Northerners who have upset the balance of status relationships in the South. His choice of words—"enticed off"— sexualizes the imagined relationship between Dolly and the Yankee he invokes, revealing his paternalistic desire to protect her. The specter of the Yankee enables Manigault to act the parts of both the slave hunter and Dolly's protector, while Dolly is made to perform the roles of both the hunted runaway and the missing person in need of Manigault's protection.

Manigault's desire to make Dolly stop running and become his property once again is expressed most powerfully by the inclusion of her photograph in the notice. Framed by the camera, Dolly has been effectively frozen, stopped, immobilized. By including Dolly's photograph in the notice, Manigault puts the possibility of her arrest on display. Beyond its practical value as an instrument of capture, Dolly's photograph stages Manigault's fantasy of containment. Photography produces a picture of Dolly, which allows her likeness to be held and kept, thereby enabling the fantasy of possessing her. Perhaps this is why Manigault decided to keep the notice; he wanted to retain the virtual image of Dolly's capture even, and especially, if it would never be realized. And yet Dolly's image strikes the viewer as a just representation of the fugitive insofar as it oscillates between signifying Dolly's capture and signifying her escape. The image promises the reality effect of photographic detail, but its faded, incomplete, and slightly out-of-focus surface disappoints. The image performs Dolly's escape at the level of representation. It marks what Manigault's words tell: she got away.

Portraits of Slavery

Manigault's placement of Dolly's photograph in the runaway notice explicitly articulates slave imagery not only to bourgeois practices of home security but also to the photographic practices of the police in the United States during the nineteenth century and thereafter. It is not enough to say that visual implements of the American criminal justice system such as the wanted poster and mug shot have been used disproportionately to discipline African Americans. The modern-day wanted poster grew out of vernacular practices of posting in the American South, which supported the institution of slavery by facilitating commercial transactions involving human chattel and reinforcing an informal system of slave surveillance.

In the photograph Dolly is dressed fastidiously. According to custom, she wears a kerchief to cover her hair. From what's left of the image, the viewer can only make out the schoolgirl collar on her faded, plaid dress. The back of the chair on which she sits is barely visible behind her. Notably, she is photographed indoors. All of these details give her an air of composure and make the image seem more like a portrait of an individual than photographic evidence. And yet the fact that Dolly's image has been violently cropped cuts against this reading. The portrait has become a makeshift mug shot in which only her head and shoulders remain. The image appears small—not in the sense of a miniature, which fascinates with its tiny details, but in the sense of being reduced. Manigault's cut frustrates the viewer, as he has sacrificed detail for geometry. Dolly takes up a mere one-fourth to one-third of the squat rectangular image.

Dolly is shot in the frontal style of ethnographic portraits made in the 1850s. These images were intended to reveal the putative hierarchical relationship among the races, to picture the theory of the Great Chain of Being. It is quite possible that her photographer was influenced by the work of J. T. Zealy, a man who ran studios in Columbia, South Carolina, and Petersburg, Virginia. In 1850 Zealy was commissioned to produce front, side, and back views of slaves from a North Carolina slave plantation. The

Jack (frontal), 1850s. (Courtesy Peabody Museum of Art,
Archeology & Ethnology, 35-5-10/53043;
photograph by J. T. Zealey)

photographs were requested as part of the studies of Louis Agassiz, a Swiss naturalist and the founder of Harvard's Museum of Comparative Zoology. With Zealy's photographs Agassiz hoped to provide visual proof for his theory that the races had been created separately—a theory used to rationalize slavery (Marien 40–41). In these images the photographer stripped the subjects to the waist before taking their picture.[11]

"These pictures," Allan Trachtenberg writes, "invite comparison to a group of images produced by Mathew Brady in 1846—of inmates at Black-wells Island Penitentiary." Brady's images were published to show readers how to read a criminal's head for signs of the biological sources of his

Jack (in profile), 1850s. (Courtesy Peabody Museum of Art,
Archeology & Ethnology, 35-5-10/53044;
photograph by J. T. Zealey)

unwanted behavior. Trachtenberg reminds us that Mathew Brady began
photographing criminals the same year he began his "illustrious Americans" project, a classically inspired series of great American men, their
portraits offered up as images of republican virtue during an era when the
republic's very existence was threatened.[12]

Trachtenberg argues for the common ideological function of slave and
criminal portraiture: "What slave and criminal images have in common is a
system of explanation which makes the difference between free citizen and
incarcerated criminal or enslaved black seem 'natural' and proper" (56). Of
greater significance still to this study is the fact that both image sets cultivate

a sense of distance and absolute difference between viewers and viewed—a visual relationship that carried moral as well as biological connotations in American visual cultures of the mid-nineteenth century. "The anthropometric images of Agassiz and Zealy and the phrenological pictures of Brady," Trachtenberg explains, "implicitly refer to a code of rectitude presumed to make distinct the line between right and wrong, crime and obedience, and, by extension to racial hierarchy, black and white" (58–59).

In the mid-nineteenth century many Americans wanted to believe that morality was visually encoded. With respect to criminal activity, Americans found the idea that character could be deciphered from a person's physical appearance reassuring. This meant that personal practices of looking would be enough to protect ordinary citizens from being victimized by violent criminals. With respect to the slave population, it served to rationalize the institution of slavery and its indefinite extension into the nation's future. Made and circulated in the same visual culture that produced and consumed Brady's "illustrious Americans" series, slave and criminal portraits visualized biological rationales for the exclusion of these populations from the photographic frames of civic virtue and the legal limits of national belonging.

Dolly's portrait was made and eventually circulated in a landscape of competing visual claims being made in the United States about the moral, biological, and legal status of the black body. The supporters of slavery made and circulated images of slaves that adhered to the conventions of anthropological photography: so-called scientific portraits meant to demonstrate the innate inferiority of nonwhites. At the same time abolitionists made and circulated persuasive images of two idealized slave types: the suffering and the redeemed slave. They distributed iconic images and sentimental portraits of slaves together with vivid narratives to elicit sympathy from white listeners.

In their efforts to criminalize the institution of slavery, abolitionists turned the slave into a victim of the slave owner's barbaric crimes. In response to the "scientific" racism of the anthropological mug shot, abolitionists circulated the trope and iconography of the suffering slave. During this period, Elizabeth Clark argues, the moral sense of the nation became aligned more with feeling than with rational thought (463–93). Sentimental portraits of suffering and redemption were valuable to the abolitionist movement because they prompted some whites to identify with the slave's suffering. Through the manipulation of public feelings about the allegorical slave, the way was being paved for the rational notion of universal human rights that would free actual slaves. The objectification of the slave in this manner was strategic. It was believed that most white people needed to work with the object of the suffering slave, if they were to learn to sympathize with the plight of the slave (E. Clark 479). It was not only Northerners who practiced this way of seeing slaves. Sarah Grimké enthusiastically supported the increased manufacture and distribution of such images in the South so that the "speechless agony of the fettered slave may unceasingly appeal to the heart of the patriot, the philanthropist, and the Christian" (481).

I argued earlier that the early nineteenth century saw the shift from a Puritan to a gothic structure of feeling with respect to displays of crime and punishment (see chapter 1). The same cannot be said for the structure of feeling that surrounded the slave imagery circulated by abolitionists in the mid-nineteenth century. This was not the coperformative witness and imaginative identification of a community member at a public execution, nor was it the distanced fascination with the criminal as a gothic monster. Rather, it was a feeling of pity for the racial other, inspired in the heart of a white Christian of conscience, who encountered these images at home in her parlor or perhaps at a lecture she attended. The mode of spectatorship practiced and cultivated by abolitionists was an exercise in the benign racism of condescension toward African Americans and the assumption of moral superiority with respect to white Southerners.

Abolitionist imagery and literature carried the tinge of scandal. Predicting the early twentieth-century tradition of muckraking, abolitionist narratives, testimonials, and photographs of suffering operated according to a visual logic of exposure. They opened the private traditions of the Southern plantation family to public (read, Northern) oversight and judgment. Part of the appeal of such narratives and images lay in the act of uncovering the intimate secrets of this quasi-domestic space, as well as the sense of moral superiority experienced by Europeans and Northern Americans as they looked at these images and heard these stories. In other words, abolitionist stories and images recast Manigault's protection scenario: the abolitionist would protect the slave from the monstrous slave owner.

While drawings were a popular way to represent the idealized type of the suffering slave, photographs were considered more powerful because of their status as evidence and their ability to render suffering in great detail. Before the spread of photography, the most moving evidence of the brutality of slavery was to be found in detailed oral and written accounts (M. N. Mitchell 393–95). At the height of the Romantic movement in American literature, writes Elizabeth Clark, slave narratives and testimonials performed by abolitionists on the lecture circuit provided "intimate glimpses into the tragedy of suffering that were more persuasive than reformers' didactic rhetoric" (470). Domestic literature offered the perfect exercise in sympathy, and the home was "revealed as the site of entry into private spaces and feelings that sparked the sympathetic imagination" (486).

Images such as *Scourged Back* provided Northerners with a firsthand look at the violent effects of slavery. The widely reproduced photograph of Gordon, an escaped slave, spoke volumes. It told a story to the eye that had been written in the master's hand. In the photograph of Gordon's scarred back, the viewer reads a narrative inscribed by the slave owner himself. By allowing the slave master's actions to speak through the image of the slave's body, the photograph appears to remove the mediating factor of interpretation on the part of the slave. As far as Victorian Americans were concerned, photographic images of cruelty to slaves trumped oral and written representations of abuse and torture. The photograph was felt to be a more direct communication of the truth about slavery than the accounts of torture and beatings related by the authors of slave narratives. Ultimately, though, photography was embraced not only because of its status as evidence but also because of the new forms of morbid sensationalism made possible by photographic detail.

Whereas illustrations and photographs of the suffering slave often pictured grown men, the photographic portraits of "redeemed slaves" circulated by abolitionists in the 1860s, right around the time Manigault made his poster, featured mostly light-skinned children. The logic that made such visual contrasts meaningful to Americans was a blend of Social Darwinism and Christianity. Such images relied on the viewer's subscription to a racist evolutionary scheme, which ranked Africans as the least evolved of the races and Europeans as the pinnacle of civilization, and on faith in Christianity's fondness for the white child, who was understood as the embodiment of innocence and the absence of sin.

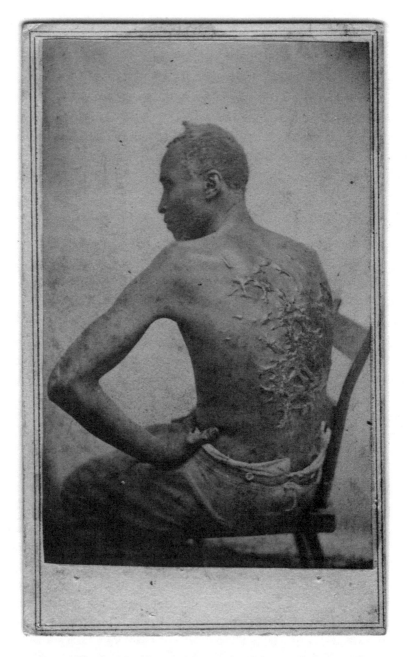

Scourged Back, 1863. (Courtesy International Center of Photography, New York City; photograph by McPherson & Oliver)

Abolitionist photographs of redeemed slaves were informed by the conventions of family portraiture and, as a result, transposed moral assumptions about the guilt and innocence of men and women-and-children, respectively, onto images of freed slaves. One series, commissioned by the National Freedmen's Association to raise funds for the newly opened Free Schools of Louisiana, featured children almost exclusively. Perhaps the adult black body was already in excess of the redeemable. Indeed, Mary Niall Mitchell argues that the racial and class coding of former slaves in these images was a political ploy meant to elicit identification from white, middle-class Northerners, who were encouraged to see a connection between the poor dears and their own children. In the guise of child portraits, abolitionist propaganda took on an air of intimacy, which allowed it to move from the public sphere into the homes of white Northerners. "With each child framed in the vignettes and parlor scenes associated with white northern middle-class girlhood," Mitchell writes, "these images of 'slave girls' brought antislavery into the homes, perhaps even the family photograph albums, of many white northerners" (379).

The suffering slave and the redeemed (often female) child were idealized types that worked in tandem: in a strange reversal the adult became the "before" to the child's "after" picture. Indeed, photography was well equipped to picture the quality of suddenness that was so appealing to Christian Americans in narratives of emancipation. This was no longer the contingent salvation of a soul on the scaffold. Rather, salvation began to resemble the social reformer's logic of the makeover, which would be well served by photography. According to Elizabeth Clark, the dramatic appeal of slave narratives lay in the suddenness of Emancipation, which was often compared to the suddenness of Christian conversion (477). Americans and Europeans alike were attracted to the dramatic clarity of slave narratives' progression from before to after, from slave to free man or woman. With its definitive *take,* photography dramatized redemption as the frozen image of a clean, well-dressed, and white-looking former slave. The freezing power of photography assured white viewers that despite the revolutionary changes taking place in the United States, the nation would remain white. Like a photograph soaked in the proper chemical solution, the nation's composition was fixed.[13]

Redeemed in Virginia

By Catherine S. Lawrence. Baptized in Brooklyn, at Plymouth Church, by Henry Ward Beecher, May, 1863. Fannie Virginia Casseopia Lawrence, a Redeemed SLAVE CHILD, 5 years of age.

Entered according to Act of Congress, in the year 1863, by C. S. Lawrence, in the Clerk's Office of the district Court of the United States, for the Southern District of New-York.

Photograph by Renowden, 65 Fulton Av. Brooklyn.

Propaganda portrait of Fannie Virginia Casseopia Lawrence, a redeemed slave child, five years of age, 1863. (Photographs and Prints Division, Schomburg Center for Research in Black Culture, The New York Public Library, Astor, Lenox and Tilden Foundations; photograph by Renowden)

Makeshift Mug Shots

Alan Sekula argues that photographs taken for police and prison records during the latter half of the nineteenth century should be seen alongside the portrait photographs that flourished at the same time. In his words, "the general all-inclusive archive necessarily contains both the traces of the visible bodies of heroes, leaders, moral exemplars, celebrities, and those of the poor, the diseased, the insane, the criminal, the nonwhite, the female, and all other embodiments of the unworthy" (10). Dolly's image is both at once: it is a family portrait, and, transformed by its placement in the runaway notice, it is an image of criminality.

Dolly's image is cut from a *carte-de-visite,* or "card photograph," as they were called in the United States. The photograph was likely made in the 1850s or early 1860s (Marien 85). While Manigault's use of the card photograph as mug shot may seem a departure from the sentimental keepsake, it is actually in keeping with the card's original purpose. A. A. Disdéri's *carte-de-visite* invention was imagined as a novel extension of the traditional calling card, designed for the growing urban societies in Europe so that the bourgeoisie might use photographic identification to screen visitors to their homes.[14] As a card photograph, therefore, Dolly's image is a provocative reminder of the historical connections between police photography and related bourgeois practices of domestic and peer surveillance.

It is likely that Manigault included Dolly's photograph not only as a tool for capturing her but also as proof of his own innocence. Deborah Willis notes that slave owners sometimes photographed their slaves in order to prove that they were healthy and well taken care of.[15] Perhaps Dolly's image, much like Manigault's verbal description of her, was meant to communicate more about him than about her. To his Southern neighbors the portrait might have communicated the message that Manigault was a benevolent father figure and that it was himself, rather than Dolly, who had been wronged. To an imagined Northern audience the inclusion of Dolly's image would have communicated Manigault's stubborn determination to reclaim what, he believed, rightly belonged to him. In both cases Manigault has used her image to say something about himself. This is Dolly's representational labor, which she performs above and beyond her cooking, cleaning, and childcare duties in the Manigault household. Photography demands more of Dolly because it makes her available to Manigault in new ways. Possessing Dolly's photograph, Manigault is able to extend her command performance of servitude into the realms of representation and history.[16]

Ironically, the slave hunter became the hunted outlaw. Emancipation effectively criminalized the institution of slavery and Manigault's practice of slave hunting. With the runaway notice Manigault resisted this state of affairs and attempted to claim Dolly's innocence for himself. His text mourns not only his personal loss of status occasioned by the Civil War and Emancipation but also the Southern white race's loss of its metaphoric, even idyllic, childhood. According to Susan Stewart, the motif of a lost childhood remade in the remembering may be found in souvenirs of individual life histories, but also in the broad "antiquarian theme of the childhood of the nation/race" (145). Souvenirs evoke memories of a childhood recreated from its material remains, not of a childhood as lived.

After the Civil War, without abolitionist didacticism or status relationships as interpretive controls for anchoring the meaning of the black body, the modes of its representation became more distanced and "objective" in the North and more visceral and pornographic in the South. The mixed-genre runaway notice was replaced in the public sphere by more clearly delineated and more extreme versions of itself: the police mug shot and the lynching postcard. Each form of representation, in turn, accompanied a new set of disciplinary practices used to expel African American men from the public sphere.[17]

No longer the remote, sentimental victims of Southern injustice, many freed blacks migrated north after the war. The increased presence of blacks in the North caused a great deal of anxiety among whites, who would have preferred to imagine blacks from a distance, like tragic characters in a novel or redeemed innocents solemnly pictured in a card photograph. These newcomers were not merely the tokens of abolitionist sentimentality or the visual "props" for a sympathetic white imaginary; rather, these were real people looking for paid work in the North. Fearful of their new neighbors, many whites marshaled the criminal-justice system against blacks. The white practice of picturing and collecting blackness continued through the practices of the professional police. Images of the suffering slave morphed into "mug shots" of particular suspicious persons, underlining the power and authority of professional organizations to survey and protect (white)

Police mug shot of Benjamin Rutledge, "Suspicious Person,"
1901. (Courtesy Derrick Beard)

society. In the North the blackness of a suspect's skin was not overtly given as the reason for his or her guilt, only counted as part of a general aura of dangerousness. In police practice the racialized gaze was insulated by the institutional protocols to which it conformed. The attribution of guilt to freed blacks in the North became a matter of captioning—the rationalization for an arrest scrawled on the back of a photograph: "suspicious person."

Souvenirs of White Supremacy

In the South the predominant image of white supremacy was not the police mug shot, but the lynching postcard. After Emancipation freed blacks were no longer useful as "credits" to their masters. African Americans could no longer be understood as expressions of their master's kindness, generosity, discipline, ferocity, and so on. The deep frustration and madness that this representational crisis caused among some whites are attested to by both the indiscriminate waves of violence committed against blacks and the regional production and mass circulation of lynching images. During Reconstruction lynching served not only to terrorize African Americans but also to express regional resistance to national rule. Macabre tokens of white supremacy were made and circulated—as if trophy photos could counteract the freed man's or woman's uncanny embodiment of what the South was missing.

Historians point to the American social reforms of the nineteenth century as the beginning of the end of public execution in the United States.[18] However, the history of lynching suggests that many whites held onto a tradition of spectacular torture featuring the black body.[19] The late nineteenth century was a time of zealous recommitment to the gore and brutality of the public execution among white Southern evangelical Protestants.[20] Lynching was understood as a ritual means of achieving the racial and spiritual purification of the community, in so far as racial identity and moral character were directly aligned. Peter Ehrenhaus and Susan Owen argue that the explanation for the rise of lynching, as other types of public execution decreased, "is not found in a retreat from Christian doctrine, but in its embrace" (277).

Racist interpretations of Christian doctrine provided a rationalization and aesthetic for exclusionary practices that were fundamentally motivated by the political and economic threats that freed blacks posed to whites. The spectacle of lynching served simultaneously to terrorize blacks and to reassure whites. Robyn Wiegman argues that lynching was a means of securing the differences between white and black men at a time when Emancipation threatened to erode those differences. The black man's threat, she writes, "arises not simply from a perceived racial difference but from the potential for masculine sameness" (90).

Lynching was, therefore, a gendered response to the threat of political castration by Emancipation and black suffrage. It mattered not that the practitioners of lynching were, in most cases, not dispossessed former slave owners. Lynching was a continuation of poor whites' work as helpmates to wealthy planters, who desired and actively cultivated racist sentiment as a means of encouraging systematic surveillance of their private property. Jacquelyn Dowd Hall explains how lynching continued as a remnant of vigilantism that long outlasted the system's formal replacement by the professional police: "Rather than passing with the frontier . . . lynching was incorporated into the distinctive legal system of the southern slave society" (329). The terrorizing effects of lynching were extended through whites' practices of documenting and reproducing the scenes of torture.[21] As Leigh Raiford persuasively argues, lynching was a "peculiarly modern phenomenon, reliant on various communication, transportation, and especially media and consumer technologies" (267). The reproduction of lynching photographs on mass-produced postcards made them into commodity fetishes that could be purchased for a modest fee. As such, lynching postcards reinforced the primitive function of group violence through modern acts of individual consumption—a founding contradiction in American visual culture that remains operative in the vigilante viewer.

CHAPTER THREE

Pinkerton Posters

OVER THE LATTER HALF OF THE NINETEENTH CENTURY, violence was officially made the exclusive provenance of the professional police. Detectives based out of Northern cities claimed the practice of fugitive display for the work of catching criminals. During this nascent era in American policing, urban attitudes toward the work of detection vacillated between desire for police protection and suspicion of the professional police. Many people felt that detection ran counter to what it meant to be an American, understood as marked by "openness, candor, forthrightness and trust" (Morn 68). Anti-spy and anti-police attitudes grew out of Americans' distrust of big government and their desire to avoid the excesses of the English and French police systems. Americans differentiated themselves by opting to rely on older, communal methods of keeping the peace and openly embraced a certain degree of disorganization as protection against the formation of a police state. As a result, public police forces were not established in major cities until the urban riots at midcentury.[1] Up to that point ordinary citizens had been responsible for the prevention and detection of crime.

The spread of photography in the 1840s and 1850s

was coincident with the spread of the popular sciences of phrenology and physiognomy, interpretive systems for reading the surface of the body as a series of signs expressing inner character (Henning 221). During these years it was not uncommon for Americans to purchase manuals that instructed them in the art of detecting the moral righteousness or decrepitude of complete strangers. Although personal detection manuals typically stressed the public's role as helpmate to the police, Jennifer Green-Lewis writes, they were actually intended as defenses against the professional police's encroachments on urban space (203). Personal detection guides reinforced popular belief in the notion that the body and photography would reveal a person's true nature—indirectly suggesting that the public did not need the police. With practice persons in the know could mitigate the vulnerabilities produced by urban anonymity and therefore go on policing their own communities.

The Rogues' Gallery

In this cultural context the rogues' gallery served as a transitional space between community and professional policing. Ordinary Americans visited detective offices, where they consumed outlaw displays curated by the professional police. But their practices of looking were variously understood as a popular form of amusement and as an invitation to practice the art of detection as a personal safety strategy. These uses of the rogues' gallery thrived, despite the fact that the initial rationale for its establishment focused on the gallery's instrumental function.

In 1857 Police Sergeant William H. Lefferts suggested that a photo gallery be established in the detective office of the New York City police (Green-Lewis 201-3). The gallery would be open to the public and made available to the victims of crime so that they might identify their assailants. Within a few years, however, the rogues' gallery was understood as an exhibition appropriate for the public at large. In 1859 the *American Journal of Photography* published an article entitled "The Rogues' Gallery," which detailed the collection of criminal photographs kept and exhibited by the New York City police. The article explained the merit of this new visual technology in terms of public safety: "As soon as a rascal becomes dangerous to the public, he is taken to the Rogues' Gallery, and is compelled to leave his likeness there, and from that time he may be known to any one." Within the rogues' gallery's technology of display, visibility was punishment. According to this early essay, the keepers of the collection rewarded criminals who promised to reform themselves by turning their pictures toward the wall (Trachtenberg 28–29).

Rogues' galleries spread to other American cities and quickly took up space in the public imagination. Tom Gunning compares the rogues' gallery to the era's other popular amusements: "The public display of portraits of professional criminals (who sought anonymity and concealment) became one of the most popular forms of photographic galleries, with tourists flocking to them as an urban sight and Barnum displaying them in his museum" (24). Like Barnum's museum or Mathew Brady's studios, rogues' galleries "were places to stroll, to allow people a change of pace from the crush of the street—places to see and be seen" (Trachtenberg 39). It was not only the outlaw who was monitored as a result of being mugged in the "hall of fame"; viewers' interactions with his image were also subject to public oversight. In addition to being an invitation to criminal identification, then, the rogues' gallery also provided an opportunity to be seen contemplating images of outlaws.

Displaying sets of outlaws, all in a row, the rogues' gallery cultivated a tourist's gaze in visitors to the police station or detective's office. It functioned as an exhibitionary complex in which mobile spectators paraded by the outlaws exhibited for their viewing pleasure, while other visitors watched their practices of looking.[2] Exposure to public-safety pedagogy was the price of admission to this popular form of entertainment. According to Green-Lewis, "The gallery would remind visitors that the individual should be vigilant in the crowds of the city. The public would become its own detective" (203). But this phase in the history of outlaw display was short-lived. In 1866 the New York City Police Department had to close its gallery to the public due to the overwhelming crowds of visitors. The authorities declared that any member of the public wishing to view police photographs must have a compelling reason (Green-Lewis 206).

Public access to criminal photographs remained relatively limited in New York City until the 1866 publication of *Professional Criminals of America* by Inspector Thomas Byrnes, the head of the detective offices of the New York City Police. This lavish book, which featured over two

Rogues' Gallery, New York City Police Department, 1909.
George Grantham Bain Collection. (Courtesy Library of
Congress, Prints and Photographs Division)

hundred mug shots, was addressed to professional and popular readers alike. It promised to make the work of detection more efficient for professionals, and it promised the public self-protection against criminals. In the book's preface Byrnes expresses his reasons for compiling the book and his utopian aspiration that its publication would put an end to crime:

> As crimes against property are of so frequent occurrence in the cities and towns of this country, it was suggested to my mind that the publication of a book describing thieves and their various ways of operating would be a great preventative against further depredations. Aware of the fact that there is nothing the professional criminals fear so much as identification and exposure, it is my belief that if men and women who make a practice of preying upon society were known to others besides detectives and frequenters of the courts, a check, if not a complete stop, would be put to their exploits. While the photographs of burglars, forgers, sneak thieves, and robbers of lesser degree are kept in police albums, many offenders are still able to operate successfully. But with their likenesses within reach of all, their vocation would soon become risky and unprofitable.

Byrnes explicitly distances himself from the popular sciences of phrenology and physiognomy, stating that he does not believe character can be read from the surface of the face: "Look through the Rogues' Gallery and see how many rascals you find there who resemble the best people in the country" (209).

Up to this point the question of whether police photography would primarily serve classificatory or individualizing practices of looking had remained unsettled. Byrnes clearly held the latter view, but even in cases where the authorities share criminal photographs for the express purpose of identification, the practice of outlaw display encourages a classificatory look. After all, Byrnes presents criminals in a series, offering them up to the viewer as a complete set: *Professional Criminals of America.*[3] The continued cultivation of classificatory reading practices meant that even as police photography came to be understood as a technology of identification, the characteristic tension between photography's individualizing and typological impulses continued to shape public reception of official outlaw displays.

The Modern Detective

In the absence of a federal police force, Pinkerton's National Detective Agency played a prominent role in law enforcement throughout the United States during the latter half of the nineteenth century. As a result, Pinkerton's found itself beholden to the public, even though, for the most part, the private agency did not earn its keep by them. Initially, Allan Pinkerton created his detective agency in order to provide a service to railroad companies in the Midwest. Established during an era when America's technological prowess and manufacturing output outstripped its administrative capacity, Pinkerton's National Detective Agency arose to help maintain order by making sure that private property did not get lost as it was transported across the country.

One of the greatest practical problems of the nineteenth century was keeping track of people and things as both became increasingly mobile. Modern accountancy and administration practices emerged in response. So did the work of detection. The new managerial class was charged with keeping track of the wealth and property moving across the country every day, as well as administering the swelling ranks of employees required to transport goods and people.

By midcentury ongoing problems with employee theft and embezzlement meant fierce battles between railroad management and labor. The laws in existence at the time were unable to deal with the advantage that those legally charged with moving goods might take.[4] In February of 1855, after consulting with six Midwestern railroads, Allan Pinkerton created a private agency for the purpose of surveying railroad employees. His agency was to serve as the "invisible eye" linked to the "visible hand" of the professional managerial class (Morn 24). Shortly thereafter Pinkerton was also hired by the Chicago post office to stop mail robberies, to keep Washington informed about the operation of local offices, and to check on the honesty of postal workers (Morn 23).

In 1871 Pinkerton commissioned the company's insignia, the all-seeing eye, and generated a motto indicating vigilant watchfulness: "We Never

Pinkerton's National Detective Agency logo, 1870s.
(Courtesy Library of Congress, The Pinkerton Collection,
Manuscripts Division)

Sleep."[5] Cleverly, Pinkerton's motto played on popular nostalgia for the vigilantism that the agency was displacing. It was Pinkerton's, not members of the public, that must be watchful. Perhaps it is not surprising then that while Pinkerton possessed the largest private collection of criminal portraits in nineteenth-century America, he was not in the habit of sharing his photos with the public. Pinkerton wanted to professionalize the work of detection, which entailed sharing less information with the public, rather than more. In Pinkerton's words, "secrecy is the chief strength that the detective possesses beyond that of the ordinary man" (*General Principles*).

Pinkerton used promotional materials to appeal to his wealthy clients and the private companies for which he worked. However, playing up an association between his agency and perpetual surveillance wasn't without risk. In public readings the all-seeing eye could always be interpreted as an evil eye turned on the ordinary citizen, and the motto "We Never Sleep" might sound like a threat to the cherished privacy that made average Americans feel they could rest, free of the invasive eyes of the new private and public police that many rugged individualists were loathe to accept.

In 1878 Pinkerton penned the *General Principles,* in which he committed his vision of the professional detective to paper.[6] In the text he makes a historical argument for why the work of detection must be professionalized. It was necessary for detectives to become professionals, Pinkerton wrote, because "crime itself has become more scientific." In Pinkerton's opinion the modern criminal possessed an almost scientific understanding of the new banking, postal, railroad, and express systems, which allowed him to turn them to his own benefit. Unprecedented levels of organization made bigger heists possible, rendering individual crimes more dramatic and granting individual criminals notoriety. The modern criminal was developing new, more effective techniques for taking advantage of honest folks. Pinkerton argued that catching this new criminal, with his scientifically proven methods, would require a modern detective. In Pinkerton's estimation it was the job of the private detective to make his craft as "scientific" as that of the professional criminal. As he saw it, the detective was only doing what he must to catch up with the modern criminal.

In the opening statement of *General Principles,* Pinkerton introduces a new profession: "The character of the Detective is comparatively new." He goes on to distinguish the "modern detective," a professional, from his forerunners, the *mouchards* of Paris, the Bow Street Runners of London, and the "shadows" of the American police. These, he declares, "have passed away before the enlightened intelligence of modern times." Pinkerton distinguishes modern, professional detection from the rough, cynical, and "money-grubbing" bounty-hunter system practiced by free agents, rumored to be just as wild as the criminals they hunted down. Pinkerton's, in contrast, collected a fee for its services from the privately owned banks, railroads, and express companies it represented.

Pinkerton men would be above the bounty system because they would have the financial security and respect that accrues to professional men. The agency would discipline the rogue out of the detective by offering him an honest, dependable wage. In order to ensure a visible class distinction between these two characters, Pinkerton carefully monitored his employees' behaviors and habits both on and off the clock. The Pinkerton operative was to be, above all else, clean. He was not allowed to use alcohol; had a strict curfew; often slept in apartments located in the same building as the agency; and was governed by rules restricting what types of people he could associate with, when he could associate with them, and what the character of those associations should be.

In *General Principles* the work of detection becomes akin to the priesthood: "The profession of the Detective is a high and honorable calling. Few professions excel it. He is an officer of justice and must himself be pure and above reproach." Much like priests, detectives were supposed to witness and hear the confession of sins, without themselves falling prey to temptation. In the rules governing the work of detection, Pinkerton calls his men to guard against contamination by their relations with the underworld. This point is driven home in the third of the rules governing detective work: "Whenever it shall become necessary for the Detectives to apparently put on the garb of crime, in order that they may be enabled to affiliate with, and become the confidants of, the criminal, they must ever keep uppermost in their minds that there is an absolute necessity for them to maintain their integrity and manhood" (36).

In order to be effective at his work, the modern detective was required to cloister himself. Secrecy allowed the detective to do his work efficiently, but it also gave Allan Pinkerton tighter control over the agency's public image. Pinkerton, in *General Principles,* makes a strong case for the high value his agency placed on secrecy: "The power of the Detective can best be exercised when he is entirely unknown. His efficiency is thereby increased, and the risk of personal danger diminished. In proportion as this is the case, he is valuable to the Agencies, and in so far as he becomes known, his value is lessened. The Detective will, therefore, promote the interests of the Agencies, advance his own professional standing with the same, and ensure his personal safety, by using every precaution to keep *strictly secret* his connection with the Agencies" (40). In Allan Pinkerton's estimation a detective's ability to keep his identity secret translated directly into his economic value to the agency.

Not only was the Pinkerton operative charged with keeping his identity secret, but his work of collecting information was closely supervised. Allan Pinkerton enforced strict control over information collection and sharing within the agency.[7] The detective, sworn to secrecy in terms of the content and character of his work, was further commanded to guard the tricks of the trade. Part of the work of establishing detection as a profession involved creating a new form of expertise and, consequently, a new expert. The Pinkerton operative had to claim a special knowledge of the criminal that the general public lacked. In order to keep the division clear between insider and outsider, professional and layman, it was necessary to keep the tools of the professional detective out of the hands of the masses (Marvin 5). As an object the *General Principles* rulebook played an important role in securing this division. From the moment of its publication, Allan Pinkerton made a secret fetish of the book. It was agency policy to give one copy to each branch, stamped "property of Pinkerton's," along with the date of issue and the name of the city office to which it had been issued. The stamp also instructed the reader that the book was not to leave the office and that it was to be kept in a locked drawer in the superintendent's office when not in use. Needless to say, this rulebook was off-limits to the general public.

So too were the missing- and stolen-property notices circulated by the agency. Throughout the second half of the nineteenth century, the text-only reward notice served as a tool for Pinkerton's work of reclaiming stolen property. In the hands of Pinkerton's and the new managerial class, the reward notice became a communications tool for professionals only. As such, it was detached from its roots in local newspapers, where, for a fee, individuals could post their own wanted or missing advertisements. In effect, Allan Pinkerton and his peers claimed the practice of posting for the professional detective and manager. This development in the life of the text—taking the missing notice out of the hands of the individual property owner and making it the provenance of professional detective agencies— coincided with movements across the country to replace communal peace-keeping with a standing, professional police force.

No longer directed at a local readership, the reward notice temporarily became a text intended for professionals only: the merchants and movers of wealth and communications, such as bankers, jewelers, postal carriers, express companies, railroad employees, and the police. The new and newly limited audience for the poster implied a new kind of text—less expressive, less personal, and dominated by numbers, reflecting what James Carey has called the "statisticalization of the mind: the transformation of the entire mental world into quantity, and the distribution of quantities in space so that the relationship between things and people becomes solely one of num-bers" (222).[8] Like the runaway notices that preceded them, early Pinkerton notices aimed to recover stolen property, but there are no photographs in the early notices included in the Pinkerton collection, which go back to 1868. The most prominent element of these notices is not someone's face, but a long list of numbers—the serial numbers of stolen stocks, bonds, and bank notes. These notices make no mention of the robbers or bank sneaks who stole the materials. There are no physical descriptions listed of the

EXPRESS ROBBERY

NOTICE.

Office of the Adams Express Company,
Cincinnati, May 28th, 1868.

The following is a Description of some of the property stolen from this Company on the occasion of the seizure of the Express Train of the Jeffersonville Railroad Company, near Seymour, Indiana, on the night of the 22d instant:

United States Seven-Thirty Notes.

Nos. 143,625, 143,626, 143,627, 143,628, 143,629, 143,630,
Of Second Series, issued under Act of March 3d, 1865.

Also, Nos. 4,446, 4,447, 4,448, 4,449, 4,450, 4,451, 4,452,
Of Third Series, issued under Act of March 3d, 1865.

All the above Notes are for One Thousand Dollars each, and are each endorsed thus: "Pay Secretary of the Treasury for redemption. W. Mann, Cashier."

United States Seven-Thirty Bonds of $50 Each.
Dated July 15th, 1865.

Letter A.	Letter B.	Letter C.	Letter D.
No. 29,125	No. 29,126	No. 17,967	No. 164,048
89,509	26,194	101,955	164,116
115,457	102,086	150,227	224,508
164,093	161,194	161,095	333,940
228,029	85,962	321,263	

United States Seven-Thirty Bonds of $100 Each.
Dated July 15th, 1865.
All of Letter C.

No. 3,441	No. 172,040	No. 232,098	No. 336,767
3,448	172,048	220,856	470,140
37,209	172,225	232,646	471,391
103,595	172,343	232,800	471,962
103,596	172,470	234,571	196,893
122,207	183,913	254,151	
115,948	178,846	253,816	

UNITED STATES SEVEN-THIRTY BOND OF $500, LETTER D., No. 9006.

United States Seven-Thirty Bonds of $1,000 Each.

Letter A.	Letter C.	Letter D.
No. 48,837, June 15.	No. 6,207, July 15.	No. 24,900, June 15.
	6,213, July 15.	
	6,216, July 15.	48,840, June 15.
	48,838, June 15.	
	48,839, June 15.	

Compound Interest Notes—Three Years.

Letter A.	Letter B.	Letter C.	Letter D.
No. 4,996, $100	No. 56,650, $10	No. 160,298, $10	No. 16,769, $50
24,291, 50	89,307, 10		44,737, 10
26,645, 10	148,829, 10	44,805, 20	51,686, 20
46,488, 20		146,123, 10	90,513, 10
52,642, 10			
52,639, 10			

Treasury Notes, Bearing 5 per Cent. Interest.

Letter B.	Letter C.	Letter D.
No. 2,136 for $100	No. 885 for $50	No. 2,146 for $50
7,217, 50		
73,575, 20		
73,566, 20		
104,116, 20		
66,837, 10		

Coupons—From Bonds of Hardin County, Ky.
Payable at the Mercantile Bank, New York.

No. 158, for $30, Due October 1, 1867.
No. 158, for $30, Due April 1, 1868.
Nos. 399 and 400, for $3 each, Due October 1, 1867.

No. 17, for $30, Due October, 1867.
No. 17, for $30, Due April, 1868.

Mutilated Currency.

A considerable amount of mutilated Greenbacks and National Bank Notes and Postal Currency being returned for redemption in exchange.

☞ All persons, firms and corporations are hereby cautioned against receiving or negotiating the above described Bonds, Notes and Coupons, as the same were stolen, and this Company claims the right to recover their possession, whenever and wherever they can find the same.

Any person to whom any of this property may be offered will subserve the ends of justice, and much oblige this Company, by causing the arrest of the party offering the same, and advising either of the following persons, immediately, by telegraph:

HENRY SANFORD, General Superintendent, New York.
ALFRED GAITHER, Manager, Cincinnati.
ALLAN PINKERTON, Chicago.

Express Robbery Notice, 1868. (Courtesy Library of
Congress, The Pinkerton Collection, Manuscripts Division)

guilty persons. All of this suggests that the professional people and merchants in need of Pinkerton's services were more interested in the quick recovery of stolen goods than in lengthy prosecution proceedings (Morn 14).

Romancing the Outlaw

After Allan Pinkerton's death in 1884, the agency's center of power shifted from Chicago to New York, where Allan's son Robert Pinkerton presided. Due to massive striking, industrial owners and managers increasingly "equated crime and disorder with collective bargaining and work stoppages" (Morn 93). As labor strife erupted across the country, Robert Pinkerton seized on the conflicts as an opportunity for agency expansion.[9] Answering to the needs of management, just as his father had, Robert Pinkerton offered new services through the agency, including guarding industrial property and strikebreaking. Playing on middle-class fears of labor radicalism, Pinkerton's articulated its work during this period as making America safe from Communism. Between 1877 and 1892 Pinkerton's was involved in seventy strikes, most of which occurred during the 1880s.[10] Throughout the decade and into the early 1890s, there were numerous instances of Pinkerton guards shooting and killing laborers (Morn 99–100).

Public opinion was divided on the matter of Pinkerton's role in labor unrest. On the one hand, it was widely believed that Pinkerton guards provoked peaceful protesters and instigated riots by throwing the first punch, so to speak. Many working people felt that Pinkerton's preyed upon the tension typical of a strike and instigated trouble, making it impossible to strike peaceably. On the other hand, those who defended the private police said they were necessary because the public police were inadequate to keep order. Looming large in this rationale was the threat of chaos and anarchy embodied by the worker on strike. For those who supported Pinkerton's and other private police agencies, the striking laborer was the character who inspired fear and derision. Increasingly, the laborer on strike was equated with the outlaw.

During this highly controversial period in the agency's history, Robert's brother William, who headed up the Chicago office, traveled west. While passing through Spokane, Washington, he purchased a souvenir: a watercolor of a bandit who was legendary in those parts for his "hold-up" style of robbery. In a move that reversed the standard American narrative of a civilized Easterner traveling to the Wild West, William Pinkerton carried the Western outlaw back from Spokane to New York City, where he displayed the portrait prominently in the agency's headquarters. Given the historical context of his discovery, William Pinkerton's move was perhaps both sentimental and strategic. The bandit represented his father's legacy and the first era of Pinkerton's operations. But the bandit would also provide a story of origin for the agency that conveniently sidestepped its violent antilabor history. In effect, William Pinkerton's reclamation of the bandit during this period amounted to a substitution of one popular association for another. William Pinkerton stressed the detective's relationship to the bandit at a moment when Pinkerton men were aligned with the less savory characters of the petty security guard, the violent armed guard, and the traitor scab.

Indirectly, Pinkerton's used outlaw imagery against the manual laborer. During this period the agency supported the laborer's alienation and erasure under the insatiable demands of industrial capitalism, while it made visible the romantic outlaw character of an era that was on its way out. The workingman remained a silent participant in this drama, befitting his anonymity under the new relations of production. His was not a story that the agency would choose to tell; instead, the agency manipulated a bygone or disappearing image full of nostalgia. In a brilliant public relations move, the agency donned the mask of banditry, thereby publicly aligning itself with the romance of a popular rebel who acted as an acceptable surrogate for the real enemy: organized labor.

Over the coming years Pinkerton's would make much of the bandit's portrait, as well as the story behind the painting.[11] The story goes something like this: In the late nineteenth century a masked highwayman became known around the Western states for his novel style of robbery called the "hold-up."[12] He would rush suddenly into the gaming room of a gambling house in the Old West and yell, "Hands up!" while covering the players and employees with his pistol. When a bank in Reno, Nevada, was held up in this manner, locals suspected a stranger who'd been milling around town. The evidence against the stranger was that he owned a pistol similar to the one used in the hold-up, he was carrying a large supply of gold coins, and he would not tell the authorities what he was doing in Reno. The stranger was arrested and tried for the robbery.

At the trial the bank's proprietor and other witnesses attempted to identify the stranger as the bandit. When cross-examined by the defense attorney, the proprietor and his employees, known to be skilled gun fighters, were asked why they had not resisted the masked man. Each of the bank men, in turn, testified that he had been unable to draw his gun on the masked man because the bandit had never taken his eyes off of him. Each bank man was thoroughly convinced that the bandit would have shot him dead if he had so much as reached for his gun. The defense attorney made a mockery of their testimony, getting the case dismissed on the grounds that one man could not possibly have covered a dozen people at the same time.

According to Pinkerton's version of the story, a cowboy artist from Spokane was in attendance at the trial. Inspired by the courtroom theatrics, he created a watercolor portrait of the masked man, an old scout and trapper living in the area serving as the artist's model. The finished product was a three-quarter portrait of a masked man pointing a gun and staring menacingly out at the spectator. The "cowboy artist" had realized the incredible testimony of the bank men through a clever trick: the portrait's spectators would stand in for the crowd of people being held up by the bandit. The trick worked. No matter how many people cast their gaze upon the watercolor, the masked man seemed to be watching and covering them all with his gun.

When it was finished, the painting was displayed for locals at the popular Owl Café in Spokane, where William A. Pinkerton is said to have discovered it some time in 1880s.[13] There are a number of discrepancies in the *Hands Up* story, which also changes a bit from the version in the Pinkerton agency's circa-1920 promotional materials to the present-day story told on Pinkerton's Web site.[14] No matter. In both versions of the story, Pinkerton's claims further important connections to the painting: supposedly, the stranger tried for the robbery in Reno was in fact a Pinkerton operative. The detective was in a tight spot in Spokane. He couldn't very well exonerate himself in court without also jeopardizing the case on which he was working. So the Pinkerton man bravely endured his trial, thereby proving his loyalty to the agency and to his profession. In company

Hands Up, Pinkerton's National Detective Agency Publicity Materials, 1929. (Courtesy Library of Congress, The Pinkerton Collection, Manuscripts Division)

literature Pinkerton's included a self-congratulatory mention of the final score: later, Pinkerton's caught "the real masked man" and sent the scoundrel to prison for twenty long years.

At some point between the painting's discovery in the 1880s and 1920, Pinkerton's went so far as to copyright the watercolor and the story.[15] Over the coming years the agency found clever ways to exploit the connection between the bandit and the detective in the popular imagination, even as it maintained a fundamental difference between the two characters. In the agency's keeping *Hands Up* became a double portrait: of the hypervisible bandit who threatens public safety and of the invisible Pinkerton operative quietly performing his duties in order to safeguard the spectator. Through copyrighted captioning Pinkerton's remade a portrait of a rogue in its own image, introducing a second character onto the scene: the Pinkerton operative. In the watercolor the two characters share one body, giving the impression that the storied Pinkerton operative stares out from behind the bandit's mask. The Pinkerton agent was thus identified with the outlaw, accruing the cachet obtained by the criminal without criminality. There was also a powerful inversion at work: Pinkerton's turned the pervasive gaze back on the outlaw, thus appropriating the outlaw's "magical" capacity to see and so to freeze everyone—indeed, to arrest them.

While Allan Pinkerton was careful to distinguish the modern professional detective from the bounty hunters who preceded him, his sons appropriated the cowboy's image of rugged authenticity, which was never really his to give away. In *The Arcades Project* Walter Benjamin writes about the popular literary model of the noble savage: "This model of the noble and legendary savage, ingested by the American hero, repeats itself in nineteenth-century adaptations of Cooper's works, for both the Parisian detective—urban spectator par excellence, also the *flâneur* with an industrious gleam—and the Parisian criminal are based upon models of the 'good' and 'bad' savage." In the U.S. context the American detective is not necessarily an urban spectator. In his most romantic version he is the man who is able to go undetected in rural communities of the middle and far West—a man of the frontier. In the history of the American wanted poster, the primary act of image consumption—the American hero ingesting the noble savage—is repressed, such that only the modern detective's secondary act of image consumption—the Pinkerton man swallowing the bandit (who swallowed the bad savage)—becomes agency lore. Only the secondary act of image cannibalism shows through: the Pinkerton man looks like a bandit.

In the context of Pinkerton's other promotional materials, *Hands Up* takes on additional layers of meaning. Perhaps the spectacle of the masked man allowed the agency to let the public know that this figure—the mythological bandit and, later, this or that particular outlaw—was the target of its investigations and the object of its perpetual gaze, not the worker on strike or the members of the general public. Among other things, Pinkerton's may have wanted a quick way to signal danger, as embodied in an outlaw figure endowed with magical powers. The story suggests that against this figure, the average American was utterly defenseless. *Hands Up* tells a comic story about the public's naive and irrational relationship to the outlaw. It reminds the American public that they are vulnerable and prone to lose their grip on reality in emergency situations. It suggests that the sophistication of the modern outlaw calls for an equally sophisticated detective and then delivers on this fantasy: "Have no fear. The Pinkerton men are here!"

Finally, the visual dynamic on display in *Hands Up* predicts the peculiar pleasures offered to later readers of the wanted poster by the mug shot. The painted bandit produces visual pleasure by mimicking the detective's gaze and altering its course. In the disciplinary context of the courtroom or the detective agency, the visual aggression of the painter and the detectives is trained on the bandit. In *Hands Up* the bandit reverses the disciplinary gaze such that the viewers of the painting become the objects of his stare. Trained on the viewer, the bandit's gun explodes the closed circuit of looks between subject and object. The gun functions as a third eye, a camera of sorts, incorporated into the image so that the apparatus of objectification is put on display and figured as the outlaw's weapon. Covered by the gun, the viewer becomes the object of the bandit's gaze. This pretend violence, this frozen possibility of being shot by the bandit, invites playful visual identification with the role of "victim" in the protection scenario.

It is difficult to know exactly how long Pinkerton's used *Hands Up* in its promotional and public relations materials. However, it is clear from the agency's papers that the image was still in active circulation, in one form or another, as late as the mid-twentieth century. Albert E. Koehl of Koehl, Landis and Landan Inc., a Madison Avenue advertising agency, wrote to

Pinkerton's on October 14, 1948: "Dear Mr. Dudley: Here is a photostatic copy of the art work which we are using in various of the smaller ads. Frankly, I don't see what could be done to make this look more like a gun unless we angle it a little to the right or left in which case the revolver would not be facing the 'victim.' Obviously, when this is reduced in size all of the features are made correspondingly hard to distinguish."[16] From Koehl's letter it seems that Pinkerton's was acutely aware of the visual power of the *Hands Up* image and that at some point the visual trick became insufficient to the task of selling the agency's services. From the ad executive's comments it seems that Pinkerton's had reached a point where the bandit's gun needed a gun.

The public relations work accomplished for Pinkerton's by the mythological bandit character depicted in *Hands Up* establishes the range of rhetorical functions performed by later public displays of real outlaws. Like Pinkerton's fabled bandit, later police displays of the mug shot would use the outlaw's image to steal the outlaw's magic, to reassure the public that it was not under surveillance, to signify police expertise, to remind the public of their dependence upon professionals, and to distract readers from the controversial practices and periodic excesses of a standing police force.

Tokens of Detection

In the bandit performance was duplicity, whereas in the detective it was a skilled craft and a rational act associated with a particular profession. In the early years of the detective agency, Allan Pinkerton could not afford to subscribe to the notion that you can tell a thief just by looking at him. If there were a distinct criminal type, identifiable on looks alone, then the agency would go out of business.[17] Allan Pinkerton did not associate criminal activity with biological makeup or physical appearance. As practiced by his agency, the work of detection assumed that you could never tell a thief from an honest man just by looking at him. Spying was necessary precisely because dishonest activity could be hidden by the display of honesty. Just as the detective was trained to put on "the garb of crime," so the thief was adept at putting on the garb of innocence. Apparently, the criminal had to be outed from the appearance of a hardworking American. The detective's work continued to be about seeing, but this was seeing as penetrating misleading or obscuring surfaces, seeing beyond, rather than deciphering, appearance.

It was not until after Allan Pinkerton's death in 1884 that the use of mug shots became agency policy.[18] In the development of a second-generation expert culture at Pinkerton's, the relatively young technology of photography proved essential. Claims to the agency's authority were strengthened by photography's unique purchase on reality. While a thief was often a good liar, a photograph of a thief—it was believed—could not lie. But the relationship between photography and police work was never that simple. In fact, the mug shot had to be standardized precisely because of a crisis of faith in the truth of appearances. "Contrary to the commonplace understanding of the 'mug shot' as the very exemplar of a powerful, artless, and wholly denotative visual empiricism," writes Alan Sekula, "early instrumental uses of photographic realism were systematized on the basis of an acute recognition of the *inadequacies* and limitations of ordinary visual empiricism" (18). The criminologist Alphonse Bertillon argued for an aesthetically neutral standard of representation in the mug shot because it would facilitate the work of making a positive identification. Bertillon insisted on a standard focal length, even and consistent lighting, and a fixed distance between the camera and the sitter. He took two shots: head on and profile. The profile shot was intended "to cancel the contingency of expression," since the contour of the head remained the same regardless of expression (Sekula 30).

The tension between photography's promise as a technology of capture and its limitations as an instrument with which to secure truth is materialized in the division between the front and back sides of the photographic cards collected by Pinkerton's. In the time it takes to turn a card over in your hand, you move between image and caption, photographic record and abbreviated case history, the face and the number. In addition to their instrumental power, the cards possessed a magic quality. They were a realist's charms for warding off the outlaw's endless string of aliases, lies, and stories. The cards were miniatures, secret objects meant for carrying in the detective's pocket. Photographic cards were therefore sensual tools of capture and eventually became romantic tokens of the work of detection itself.

Pinkerton's photographic identification cards feel like playing cards.

Identification card for Laura Bullion, member of the Wild
Bunch gang, 1901. (Courtesy Library of Congress, Prints and
Photographs Division)

Shuffling through them, one comes across multiple reproductions of the
same photograph. The fronts of the cards give the impression of a redun-
dancy of the image. The backs, with their discrepancies in name, occupation, state of nativity, and so on, create a different impression—of "bad
information." Take, for example, four separate cards filled out for a woman
arrested in conjunction with train and bank robberies committed by the

Reverse side of identification card for Laura Bullion, member
of the Wild Bunch gang, 1901. (Courtesy Library of Congress,
The Pinkerton Collection, Manuscripts Division)

Hole in the Wall Gang. Around the turn of the century, Pinkerton's collected a total of four photographic cards on Laura Bullion, a woman said to
have ridden with the gang for a time.[19] There is a Bertillon card from a
police station in St. Louis, where she was arrested on November 6, 1901.
There is a second Bertillon card, filled out in a separate hand and cut in half,
making it impossible to read all of her measurements, listed on the back. A

third, smaller card, made by Pinkerton's, features a frontal photograph of Bullion. Under her face is a stamp indicating that this is a "Bertillon photograph." A fourth card, also made by Pinkerton's, uses the same photograph of Bullion but does not identify the image as a Bertillon photograph.

On the reverse side of these repetitions of the same face is an endless shuffling of names, real and fake, as though it were impossible to tell the difference. On her St. Louis Bertillon card the prisoner's name is listed— Della Rose, aliases: Clara Hays and Laura Casey. On the second Bertillon card her name is given as Della Rose, her aliases as Clara Hays, Laura Casey, and Laura Bullion. On the first Pinkerton's card she is named Laura Bullion, and the aliases given are Della Rose, Clara Hays, and Laura Casey. On the second Pinkerton's card her name is listed as Laura Bullion, her aliases as Della Rose and Clara Hays. The prisoner's crime is forgery on three cards and "having stolen money" on the fourth. She is described repeatedly as a prostitute, but also once as an associate of train robbers and another time as a servant. Her state of birth, Kentucky, remains constant throughout the cards. So do her age, weight, height, and other physical descriptions. All four cards are dated with the time of Bullion's arrest, November 6, 1901, but they give no indication of whether some were made later as duplicates and, if so, when they were made.

Photographic Reward Notices

By the turn of the century, Pinkerton's was pulling photograph cards from its files and posting them on reward notices. Developments in criminology, as well as technological innovations in the mechanical reproduction of images, made it possible to reproduce the mug shot on the reward notices circulated by the agency. First, the development of the mug shot, as a cellular form of criminal portraiture, led to a new way of seeing the professional criminal as a unique individual with a particular history of recidivism. Second, French criminologist Alphonse Bertillon had invented a system for organizing police archives, which made it possible to track criminals by their history of offenses, thereby making it feasible to separate the professionals from the amateurs.[20] Third, the technological breakthrough of the half-tone plate in the 1880s made it possible to reproduce photographs on a printing press.[21]

Gold Brick Swindlers, Portland, Oregon, 1893. (Courtesy
Library of Congress, Pinkerton Papers, Manuscripts Division)

Within the archives of modern disciplinary institutions, standardization
would make photography a more effective means of identification. It drastically limited photography's powers of signification in order to make the
mug shot more purely instrumental. However, let loose in public space,
where it retained the exhibitionary trace of the rogues' gallery, the mug
shot, with its look of standardization, served the purpose of outlaw com-
modification as much or more than it signified police objectivity. Like the
promotional *Hands Up* bookmark, the mug shot substituted a commodity
form—the card photograph—for folk legend. The mug shot transformed
the legendary into currency, reflecting new forms of belonging and competition in consumer society.

The buildup of the photographic archive over the nineteenth century
made portraits of criminals significant only in their relation to other possible images and only with respect to broader systems of classification. If
the photographic image of the nineteenth century was, as Oliver Wendell
Holmes famously argued, a new universal currency, then the body became
a vehicle for the transportation and display of different looks—familial or

criminal, well-to-do or down-and-out, manly or effeminate—all of which fed back into the larger set of equivalencies established by the photographic archive as a whole.

By 1894 the *New York Illustrated News* was bold enough to expect the Pinkerton Agency's cooperation in sharing images of notorious outlaws, and they got it.[22] A newsman from the paper wrote Robert A. Pinkerton, who managed the agency's New York offices, to request the images of particular crooks whose pictures were desired by his readers. His letter documents the moment when the practice of publishing the mug shots of wanted criminals in newspapers became commonplace, creating a readership with an appetite for the stuff: "My Dear Mr. Pinkerton: Kindly let the bearer have the photos of the southern train robbers and any other *'good'* crooks you may have." The "southern train robbers" to whom the newspaperman refers were Charles J. Searcy and Charles Morganfield, who had robbed the Adams Express Company at Aquia Creek, Virginia, in 1894.

Upon receiving the newspaper's request, Pinkerton wrote to the Adams Express Company in Philadelphia, asking for the photographs. The manager promptly sent two images of Searcy to Pinkerton—"one with his hat on, and the other without." Pinkerton also wrote to the Philadelphia branch of his own agency in order to secure more information about the case. Edwin S. Gaylor, the superintendent of Pinkerton's Philadelphia office, described the circumstances surrounding the taking of the photographs, indicating Searcy's understanding that his photograph would be circulated widely and his corresponding sense of pride about his image: "The picture of Searcy showing him with a mustache was taken with a Kodak camera shortly after his arrest and while walking along the street; and the other two pictures of him were taken by the authorities at Fredericksburg VA, who permitted him to have his moustache shaved off and gave him a boutonniere" (Gaylor).[23] Searcy's desire to look his best not only reveals popular attitudes toward having one's picture taken but indicates Searcy's awareness that the picture would be seen by more than the police. It is possible that Searcy's self-consciousness reflects his longing for the glamour that was beginning to accrue to the most daring and outlandish outlaws.

Presaged in the *Hands Up* painting and other promotional materials for the agency, the photographic Pinkerton notice would soon become the public face of a business that had long kept its photographic cards tucked

Photograph of Charles Searcy taken at the time of his arrest,
1894. (Courtesy Library of Congress, Pinkerton Papers,
Manuscripts Division)

deep in its pockets. The first photographic wanted posters issued by Pinkerton's were one-sided poster versions of identification cards. Through the poster the detectives shared the contents of the card with the public, but in a flattened-out form that let readers know they still were not privy to everything. The difference between holding the card and reading the poster was the distance separating the professional from the layperson. The public could look, but they couldn't touch. The degeneration that occurred in the translation of the photographic card to the mass-produced poster paradoxically heightened the realness of the outlaw's body and the public's distance from it, as well as their difference from the modern detective.

Much of the work that has been published on Americans' fascination with the outlaw portrays popular desire for the outlaw as an act of resistance to modernization, with roots in rural folk cultures. As these narratives tell it, rural communities challenged the overwhelming and threatening forces of modernization through identification and solidarity with "social bandits"—those Robin Hood figures who took on the new, invasive systems of transportation, communication, and banking, which threatened to wipe out local economies and traditions.[24] In these treatments collective desire for the bandit is nostalgic because " 'modernization,' that is to say the combination of economic development, efficient communications and public administration, deprives any kind of banditry, including the social, of the conditions under which it flourishes" (Hobsbawm 22). Desire for the bandit is also considered an expression of social resistance to the buildup of nation-states, with their rationalized forms of violence and social control, as well as a reaction to the encroachments of outsider authority and capital.[25]

However, the history of professionally authored outlaw displays in the United States suggests that popular desire for the outlaw was never simply a reaction against modernization. Rather, the professional police and private detectives strategically cultivated and fed popular desire for the outlaw through distinctly modern practices of outlaw display. Pinkerton's obligations to the public made it no different from other nineteenth-century American businesses. The pressure to please the public was an effect of broader shifts during the nineteenth century, from a production- to a consumption-oriented society, and the attendant explosion of visual culture. In order to protect the agency's post as the first and only national detective force in the United States, Pinkerton's had to win and then maintain the public's consent. Outlaw displays answered to the power vested in the new consumer public, in its role as captive audience to private and public authorities alike. Like *Hands Up,* Pinkerton's photographic reward notices addressed readers as if they were bored tourists wandering aimlessly through a gift shop out West. To say this is merely to acknowledge that turn-of-the-century private detective posters were already souvenirs of vigilante violence.

CHAPTER FOUR

The FBI's Most Wanted

In the World War I–era wanted poster for Grover
Bergdoll with which this book opens, one can discern
traces of two distinct print genres: war propaganda and
tabloid journalism.[1] The key to their convergence lies
with Bergdoll's status as the "number-one" or "most
wanted" enemy of the United States. It foreshadows the
rather bizarre cultural practice of ordering and displaying
outlaws hierarchically that would become increasingly
popular with the American public over the first half of the
twentieth century. As a result, the text's address oscillates
between being pedagogical (i.e., making an example of
the outlaw) and being voyeuristic (i.e., making a spectacle of the worst among us). Because Grover Bergdoll is
number one, his outlaw performance is at once more
serious and more stimulating.

While it may seem strange, the practice of ranking
outlaws is merely an extension of the ordering impulse
that has characterized the photographic archive from its
earliest days. Writing about the formation of the photographic archive in the nineteenth century, Alan Sekula
argues that "every proper portrait has its lurking, objectifying inverse in the files of the police" (7). That is to
say, a system of comparison has always informed photo-

graphic portraiture. The practice of ranking outlaws with respect to one another, however, reflects a new stage in ways of looking at outlaws. A finer degree of comparison among outlaws transforms the spectator's relationship to outlaw displays. As the outlaw makes the progression from "bad" to "the worst," he seems to move even further from the vigilante viewer.

Number One

The son of a wealthy Philadelphia brewer, Grover Bergdoll was drafted into the U.S. Army on July 20, 1917. Not only did the young Bergdoll, twenty-three years old at the time, fail to report for duty, but he completely disappeared. For over two years local and federal agents searched for him throughout the United States and Mexico. While the hunt was in progress, authorities claimed that his evasion of the draft was motivated by his loyalty to Germany, where both of his parents had been born. The U.S. government and the press painted the Bergdolls as a rich, eccentric family of German nationalists. Federal agents said that Bergdoll had sworn he would never fight against his mother's native country. And residents of Philadelphia claimed that Bergdoll had contacted the local German consul in order to volunteer to fly for the German army.[2] During the hunt for Grover Bergdoll, which lasted over a period of more than two years, he became known as the "Number One Draft Dodger of the First World War."

Bergdoll was further removed from average Americans than his predecessors on the wanted poster not just because of his draft dodging or his ethnicity, but because of his wealth. In his photograph Grover wears a three-piece pinstripe suit, a crisp white shirt with a rounded collar, and a narrow necktie. He is looking up and off into the distance, with his head slightly turned. His image is compelling in the context of the poster precisely because he is so attractive and polished—there is nothing about this photograph that resembles a mug shot. In fact, Bergdoll's portrait lends glamour to the poster. Looking at him, one immediately senses that this is not a career criminal. This man looks as though he already has all the money he could possibly want.

The poster characterizes Bergdoll as an adventurous man of the times. "Grover C. Bergdoll," it reads, "a member of a wealthy Philadelphia family interested in the Bergdoll Brewing Company, left Philadelphia in August or September, 1917, since which time he has been traveling extensively throughout the country." The poster continues: "It is believed that he is constantly on the move, accompanied by a male companion. He is an expert automobile driver and aviator, and delights in exploiting his ability in both lines." The poster goes on to portray Bergdoll as a member of the nouveau riche, indirectly marking his family's immigrant status: "He is flashy and dramatic—a lavish spender of money. When entertaining, he displays a large roll of notes." Bergdoll's physical and character description makes it seem as though his vanity prevented him from fulfilling his duty to the nation.

What made Grover Bergdoll glamorous also made him offensive. Perhaps he did not think the rules applied to him—a sore note purposefully struck in the wanted poster calling for his arrest. Here was a man who had shirked his duty to the nation. To make matters worse, the newspapers portrayed Bergdoll as an incurable mama's boy.[3] The American public's attraction to Grover Bergdoll was therefore ambiguous. Their interest was interpretable either as proof of their loyalty to their nation and the cause of war (in the spirit of the dutiful citizen who takes the wanted poster seriously) or, conversely, as proof of their identification with an individual who flouted social responsibility (in the more perverse mode of the greasy-palmed reader of the tabloids). In the second case the public's interest in Bergdoll would have been seen as proof of the growing soullessness of Americans in a consumer society—a charge inextricably bound to their feminization by commercial and police discourses alike.

Public Enemies

In the interwar years experts declared that the decline in American morals embodied by Grover Bergdoll was a national trend, and they pinned it on the new consumer pleasures of the twentieth century. Civic and religious leaders blamed mass culture and consumption practices for mainstreaming what had been an exceptional attitude of the nouveau riche. Authorities expressed fears that such ready, easy, and affordable pleasures as the movies and popular magazines would breed "an emotional, feminized mass, characterized by mental lethargy, bad taste, and ignorance" (Marchand 69). Worse, mass culture was accused of producing an entirely new breed of young people, who in many ways fit the profile of Grover Bergdoll created by sensational newspaper accounts of his capture: a young man with a child's fantastic sense of entitlement, coupled with little, if any, sense of moral duty to the nation.

Degraded and déclassé, the American public was figured as the young woman shopper finding herself enthralled and disoriented by the spectacles offered to her in the marketplace. As consumers and tourists of mass culture, the public was, like this young woman, an easy mark; hence, it was up to the professional police to protect the public. In the face of the spectacular thrills of mass culture and consumer society, the federal police would remain sober and unimpressed. The specialized seeing of the police became, therefore, the discipline not to crane their necks around to look at the spectacles of mass culture, instead remaining focused upon potential criminal activity. A bargain was struck: the police would refuse to be seduced by mass culture so that the American public would be free to let itself go. In effect, the gendered protection scenario went national, creating a new relay of gazes among the professional police, the public, and outlaws.[4]

While the train robbers of the nineteenth century looked like rugged individualists and were therefore visually distinct from urban Americans, the gangsters of the interwar years and the Depression era looked more like Grover Bergdoll. In the twentieth century, David E. Ruth notes, consumption practices made it harder to tell the honest corporate man from the gangster (40–41). The prospect of class confusion and transformation through practices of consumption created widespread moral panic regarding the displacement of character by personality.[5] Popular crime narratives from the era were strongly anticonsumerist in terms of plot resolution, even as they offered up the gangster as a spectacle that provoked desire, admiration, and identification (Ruth 69).

Crime was treated as an exaggerated version of the lax morals thought to be sweeping the nation via the new pleasures available through the mass media and rampant practices of consumption. Unapologetically modern, the organized criminal was like a mirror image of the corporate American. Rather than guaranteeing the reader's progress and moral righteousness, the criminal's mug shot came to embody the underside of progress, representing those aspects of modern life that threatened to undo traditional social networks organized around family, ethnicity, neighborhood, gender, and class. Thus, Americans were susceptible not only to being ripped off or violated by the new criminal but to being led astray by him: "Indeed, the gangster of the interwar years was a 'public' enemy in two senses: a predator on the public, he was also part of it" (Ruth 2).

The criminals of the twentieth century were depicted as "public enemies" because they were considered to be scourges on the nation at large. The "public enemy" served as a proxy for working through moral panics regarding the degeneration of the American character in a consumer society (Ruth 63–86). The decadence of the age was felt to be at odds with the demands of nationalism—it was taken as evidence of a weakening or softening of the American will. Gangsters were loved and feared as figures who symbolized these contradictions. They were portrayed as more womanly than the average man, because they were vain and materialistic, and more manly than the average man, because they were capable of brutal violence. Americans communicated moral concerns through the discourses of gender, class, and nationalism and increasingly appealed to the morality of efficiency. Popular moral panics expressed in these terms created an environment ripe for J. Edgar Hoover's masculine overhaul of the FBI and the expansion of domestic surveillance.

Fingerprints

Federal policing expanded during the early twentieth century in the name of protecting the feminized "mass" toward whom true crime and romance stories were directed. According to Claire Potter, America's perceived state of feminine weakness during the 1920s set the stage for J. Edgar Hoover's masculine makeover of the federal police. Potter makes a convincing case that the failures of the anticrime agendas of the Bureau of Prohibition, associated with female moral reformers, actually paved the way for the victory of the masculinized, military enforcement model that characterized J. Edgar Hoover's police professionalization movement (3). Where Prohibition had failed to penetrate local arrangements and idiosyncrasies, Hoover's Bureau would succeed. The haphazard, inconsistent character of policing would be forced to submit to a new, ordered rationality, dictated by the Federal Bureau of Investigation.

With the expansion of federal policing over the course of the twentieth century, technologies for sorting out individuals from populations greatly augmented the filtering and ranking function of police work. Fingerprinting, in particular, revolutionized police work, splitting the practice of information collection from the work of interpretation.[6] This division of labor enabled the centralization of police power in the organizational body of the FBI. It also made it possible for the FBI's director, J. Edgar Hoover, to tighten his control over the flow of information. Indeed, one of the first things Hoover did upon taking up his post at the FBI was to consolidate all of the fingerprint records previously kept by the National Bureau of Criminal Identification and the Leavenworth Penitentiary Bureau (Hoover 209). Hoover's connection to the International Association of Chiefs of Police brought its vast collection to Washington, D.C., as well. Hoover also transformed record keeping by creating a cross-referencing system that permitted an agent "to take a single piece of information—a fingerprint, a physical description, a modus operandi—and trace it back to a whole criminal" (Potter 36).[7]

This period in the history of federal policing was characterized by a growing obsession with identifying, documenting, and verifying each individual member of the population, which led in turn to increasingly tighter controls over the collection and exchange of such information.[8] The shift from adequate to exhaustive record keeping was actualized through the indefinite expansion of the new national fingerprint database kept by Hoover at the Bureau. In 1925 Hoover addressed the International Association of Chiefs of Police (IACP) at its annual convention, identifying armed robbery as the worst problem facing rural and small-town police. He recast the local as a site of vulnerability and simultaneously positioned the federal government as its savior. Crime continued to be conceived of as a regional event, insofar as it threatened local people, but it also began to resemble a mobile scourge on the nation. It was a problem, therefore, that only the federal police were poised to confront.[9] Like a combination superhero/bird of prey, Hoover's FBI would survey the national problem of crime from on high, swooping down on local sites only when a criminal's notoriety made enough of a stir to attract national attention.

During the mid-1920s Hoover committed the federal government to administrative reforms, which, he said, would help the FBI address the issue of armed robbery. In 1925 the Dyer Act was passed, making the interstate transportation of vehicles a federal crime. It was around this time that the Bureau also began publishing national auto-theft records and statistics on "crimes of greater magnitude against persons or property" (Potter 36–37). Hoover used these reports to lobby local police and the American public for greater cooperation with the Bureau, particularly in matters of criminal identification and data sharing. For instance, on December 5, 1927, the National Crime Commission released a report to the public from the Committee on Criminal Statistics and Identification. The report argued that an efficient police system was "the best defense of organized society against crime" and that the present undeveloped status of criminal identification "constitutes a serious obstacle to police efficiency." It urged more effective cooperation by local police departments with the Division of Identification and Information of the Bureau of Investigation and recommended that central bureaus of identification be established in every state: "In our opinion state bureaus of criminal identification are indispensable units in a national system of criminal identification. It is impossible for the Federal Bureau of Investigation to do all of the work; it can, however, serve as a clearing-house for all of the 48 states. This is as much as it can or should do" ("Urgent" 116).

The central focus of the report was its argument for the extension and standardization of fingerprint identification as the key to efficient law enforcement. According to the report, "If the police are to bring a reasonable proportion of the criminals of this country before the courts of justice and to present evidence that will convict, there will have to be a great development and expansion in the machinery now used in taking and recording finger prints" ("Urgent" 116). If not through fingerprints, the report asks, "how can the recidivist be singled out for either added punishment or special corrective treatment?" It goes on to establish the thorough collection of information on a particular individual as the professional norm of social and correctional agencies: "Every social agency today insists on securing as complete a case history as it is possible to obtain before attempting to deal with an individual" (116). The report thus suggests that criminal-identification reform is necessary in order to bring local police practice up to date and in line with new federal standards.

In his 1927 address to the IACP, Hoover bragged that the Bureau of Identification and Information currently had 1,203,864 prints in its possession. But, he stressed, this was not enough: "I am very strongly of the opinion that the Division of Identification and Information is not receiving all of the finger print records which should be forwarded to it by the law-enforcement officers interested in its successful operation" ("Urgent" 116). Specifically, Hoover was concerned that local officers were transmitting fingerprints only for those criminals whose records were unknown. He wanted them to be less strategic and more systematic in the information that they shared with the Bureau.

Whereas it was difficult enough to organize the images in nineteenth-century photo archives, now the information collected on particular individuals was never enough. An insatiable drive for more data came into vogue as part of the development of prevention as a technique of police and correctional work, as well as social and mental health practices. By 1931, Potter writes, "virtually all government agencies were contributing fingerprints taken for any reason."[10] For the FBI, she continues, the collection of data in the name of fighting crime and political surveillance methods both operated according to the assumption that "every subject who could be added to the files was a potential criminal" (39).

Hoover articulated state efficiency in terms of national morality. He also made a convincing case that his morality of efficiency would serve the interests of both local law enforcement officials and the American public. When *American City* magazine asked J. Edgar Hoover how local police departments might best cooperate with the Division of Identification and Information in Washington, Hoover replied, "The best and only method of cooperation with the Division in Washington is for every law enforcement individual to record the finger prints of every malefactor who comes under his jurisdiction, and forward a copy of said finger prints to the Bureau" ("Urgent" 116). At the time Hoover's Bureau was already receiving between seven and eight hundred sets of prints a day. The transmission of criminal identification data to the Bureau of Identification in Washington, Hoover stated emphatically, "is not only a privilege, but a duty," one that local law enforcement officers owed to themselves and to their fellow officers.

The "War on Crime"

When J. Edgar Hoover declared war on crime, he assumed the president's sovereign power to declare a state of emergency, thereby nullifying public opposition to the drastic domestic surveillance measures he would impose.[11] Following the model established in the wanted poster for Grover Bergdoll, Hoover addressed the American public as though it were a homogeneous group of individuals who were on his side—the side of the crime fighters. The rhetoric of war enabled Hoover to assume and ultimately enforce a degree of conformity in the American people normally possible only during wartime. He addressed the American public as the potential or actual victims of criminal behavior, regardless of whether any connection existed. His rhetorical ploy of identifying enemies in their midst polarized the field of social relations, sharply dividing the authorities from those who were suspect and thereby setting the stage for his equation of criminal activity with anti-Americanism.

Hoover crafted the FBI's public image by manipulating Americans' vague moral anxiety about modern life. His war on crime would organize the public's resistance to and fear of the shifting social and economic landscape. It would channel public fears by attributing the risks of modern life to a new breed of criminals, namely, violent urban gangsters in the 1920s and suburban kidnappers and rural auto bandits in the 1930s. The FBI would connect the public's fear of these overtly dangerous and ungovernable bodies to general anxieties about young people not tied to family, such as working women, bachelors, and prostitutes—people who were mixing it up in urban places of leisure and consumption (Potter 57–58). Significantly, Hoover's war on crime spotlighted rural as well as urban gangsters, thereby spreading the threat of violent crime to every small town and sparsely populated county across the United States.[12]

Hoover used the rhetoric of war to shift moral responsibility for crime fighting from his constituency of local police to the American public. Average Americans were offered the pretense of an active role. In July of 1931 Hoover articulated his mission and its relationship to the American public: "Do not fix laxity of law enforcement upon the police agencies. It is the fault of the public. People no longer respect respectability. It is not disrespect for law. Our problem today is whether the forces of government or outlawry must dominate. You must be either with or against government. There is no middle ground. We must have the support of the public. Citizens of this country must become enemies of crime" (Potter 57). Hoover did not mince words; you were either with or against the FBI. By addressing the American public in this manner, Hoover attempted to eliminate the possibility of taking a neutral or merely fascinated stance toward violent crimes against persons or property.

Hoover's public relations tactic was to treat average Americans like wartime citizens doing their part on the home front. He wanted the American public to take a controlled interest in crime from a distance. Like a skilled propagandist Hoover led the public's attention in order to channel their identifications and desires according to his prerogatives. The American public had to become an "interested" audience in the double sense of the term: watching with rapt attention and rooting for a particular side.

Hoover's war on crime starred the FBI agent or "G-man" (short for government man) versus the celebrity gangster.[13] The G-man was a cut above your average American cop. As part of his work on this new character's public image, Hoover initiated reforms between 1924 and 1932. These included a dress code, which made Bureau agents recognizable as professionals who visually stood apart from local law enforcement officials. The G-man was a class act: well-educated and hard-working but never a blue blood. Created in Hoover's image, the G-man was a person who had raised himself up by his own bootstraps. Hoover's image and vision for the agency, embodied in the clean-cut figure of the G-man, appealed to middle-class notions about the legitimate grounds for material success in a democracy. Merit, education, and hard work were valued over insider connections (Potter 35). It was his "character"—honed through hard work and struggle —that would give the G-man and the Bureau he represented the moral authority necessary to justify the agency's increased power and expanded jurisdiction during the late 1920s and early 1930s. No surprise, then, that all-American conservative Jimmy Stewart played a G-man in the wildly revisionist film *The FBI Story* (1959).

Hoover's theater of war exploited the youngest, prettiest, and deadliest criminals. Playing attraction against repulsion much as the tabloids did, Hoover advertised the exceptionally wretched. These were not only enemies of the Bureau. They were a menace to society. The celebrity gangsters of the war on crime were designated public enemies, following a trend started in 1930 by the Chicago Crime Commission, which released a list of the city's twenty-eight most dangerous "public enemies." David E. Ruth notes that "journalists across the country published the list, adopted the

term, and dubbed the notorious Al Capone 'Public Enemy Number One.' "
The next year Warner Brothers released *The Public Enemy*, starring James
Cagney, assuring, Ruth argues, the designation's cultural longevity (2).

Labeling a criminal a "public enemy" is an attempt to turn the public
against the outlaw's image, so that he cannot serve as a figure of romance,
rebellion, glamour, or social banditry. The term attempts to consolidate the
celebrity gangster's audience against him, constituting a singular, uniform,
and supportive audience for police work. Yet the designation of gangsters
as public enemies also recognizes that practices of outlaw display—both
popular and official—invite fantasy. Labeling someone a public enemy is an
attempt to prevent identification.[14]

Ironically, once criminals were declared "public enemies" by the Department of Justice, Depression-era audiences became far more willing
to understand them within the tradition of the social bandit. Criminals'
Southern and Midwestern origins evoked nostalgia for frontier individualism. These gangsters embodied the drama of "the individual's fateful colli-
sion with the economy and new forms of state power" (Potter 5–6). Framed
as public enemies, the auto bandits and holdup gangs of the 1930s became
national celebrities who embodied the impossible contradictions of the
times: they grappled with the insatiable desires produced by the new mass
culture in highly competitive and stark economic times.

Identification Orders

Certainly the battle for the nation's soul—signified by the contest between
the G-man and notorious gangsters—was fought on many fronts; however,
it is fair to say that the FBI wanted poster and other Bureau publications
served as key discursive sites for this work. In Hoover's hands the wanted
poster multiplied its centers of distribution, extending its reach outward
from numerous locations in multiple directions. State bureaus were established to function as clearinghouses not only for fingerprint records submitted by police and informants from all over the state but also for reward
notices (Hoover 209).

In the newly networked United States, the outlaw who committed what
Hoover referred to as "major crimes" was posted locally. Simultaneously,
his record and wanted notice were sent to the appropriate FBI branch

office and headquarters. Created locally, wanted notices were replicated at the national level in the standardized form of the FBI "identification order," which was simultaneously posted and filed for future reference.[15] As the fugitive ran from the crime scene, his poster, and therefore the local and national police, as well as the citizenry, dogged him from several directions at once. All the while his permanent record grew in the files of the federal police.[16] In short, the outlaw's chances of escape were drastically slimmer in the twentieth century than they had been in the nineteenth.[17]

The identification order was a new type of Bureau record, first produced in the early 1930s, designed to facilitate communication among FBI headquarters, field offices, and local police. Detailed, specialized, and thoroughly coded, they were nonetheless visually attractive texts. Smaller than an eight-by-eleven sheet of paper—sized at eight by eight inches, like fingerprint cards—identification orders carried the crisp, compact appeal of index cards.

A testament to Hoover's organization, each individual card indicates the entire system to which it belongs. In the upper right-hand corner the fingerprint classification is given. The identification order number and date of issue appear in the upper left-hand corner. Further down, the crime for which the person is wanted is noted. Below the crime, a large fingerprint grid is printed. Smaller than the prints and centered on the page is a Bertillon-style double portrait of the wanted person, featuring a profile shot on the left and head-on shot on the right. While the fingerprints are the most prominent feature of the identification order, the photographs are its visual center.[18]

Going down the page, one moves from fingerprints to signature to photographs. Just to the left of the mug shots are a written description of the outlaw and a space for listing the names and addresses of "relatives." To the right of the photos, the individual's criminal record appears. Just below them is a copy of the outlaw's signature. At the bottom of the page a narrative, in paragraph form, details the individual's crime and, if applicable, his or her arrest and escape, followed by contact information. John Edgar Hoover, director, issued all notices.

Identification orders were addressed to professionals within the Bureau and perhaps to a select number of local policemen. In these texts Hoover reserved fingerprints as the special property of G-men. Fingerprints sig-

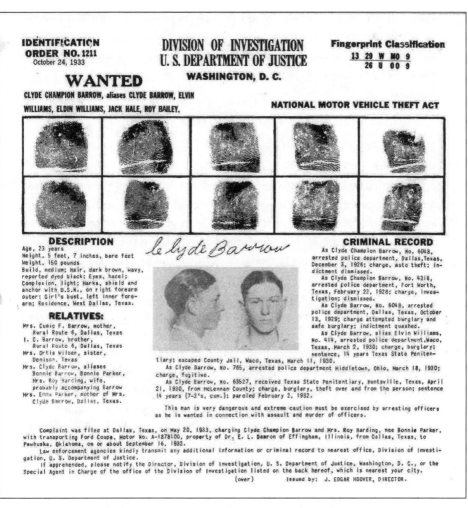

FBI Identification Order for Clyde Barrow, 1933.
(Courtesy Federal Bureau of Investigation, Washington, D.C.)

nified the technological know-how that separated the professional from the average American. While they bore an iconic resemblance to the surface of the fingertips, they did not resemble any particular person. In the age of fingerprinting face recognition became irrelevant, without the more specialized vision of the dactylographer as its guarantee. Hoover encouraged the reproduction of generic fingerprints in popular publications in order to educate the public about a process to which they might be subject but over which they would never have control. Provocatively, fingerprints signified the tension between the willful actions of the individual in the world and the body's new ability to betray itself.

Police Bulletins

Hoover continued to extend his powers over the local police by positioning them as the readership of Bureau publications. These were professional or trade journals with an instrumental purpose, but they were compiled and authored from above and dispersed at regular intervals to those below, reinforcing Hoover's power as the keeper of information, the one who was slowly becoming the author of standardized outlaw representations. With these publications Hoover tapped a constituency of local labor and created a pep club of police officers to root for the feds.

By 1932 the FBI had expanded its production of identification orders to include publications sent to the national police community on a quarterly and monthly basis: *Uniform Crime Reports* and *Fugitives Wanted by Police*.[19] *Uniform Crime Reports* collated crime statistics, created the notion of crime trends, and allowed Hoover to argue for the need for larger police forces and better enforcement (Potter 37). In the first volume of *Fugitives Wanted by Police,* published on September 1, 1932, Hoover explains why the publication had been created: "In an effort to amplify and render of increased value the current exchange of criminal identification data among the United States Bureau of Investigation and law enforcement officials in this country and abroad, it has been suggested that a bulletin be issued periodically in which will be listed data with reference to individuals for whom warrants are outstanding, and who are wanted by the law enforcement officials for major crimes" (i). Hoover admits that "major crimes" is an arbitrary designation, but one that is necessary as a place to begin. He clearly states that the bulletin is an experiment of sorts, writing that it will only continue if it proves valuable as an instrument of law enforcement.

The idea for *Fugitives Wanted by Police* arose, Hoover explains, in response to the success of the fingerprint identification system: "It is based upon the admittedly marked success which has attended the centralization of fingerprint data in the Identification Division of the United States Bureau of Investigation. It is based upon the theory that similar success will follow the establishment of a centralized division to which may be directed wanted notices by law enforcement officials everywhere in connection with fugitives whose apprehension is desired for the commission of major crimes" (i). Hoover suggests that if police work benefited from the centralization and organization of shared fingerprint data, wanted notices should be organized in a similar fashion. The primary function of *Fugitives Wanted by Police* was directing the new national traffic in wanted notices.

Published monthly, *Fugitives Wanted by Police* was comprised of brief typed entries on wanted individuals, each set off from the others by asterisks centered on the page. The entries are as brief as possible. Names are printed in all capital letters—ROY JOHN ARCHER, CLYDE CHAMPION BARROWS—and are followed by aliases; prisoner identification numbers; the institution from which the fugitive had escaped, if applicable; and race, age, height, weight, complexion, hair color, eye color, "marks," occupation, and crime(s). No gender is listed for the wanted, presumably because they were all men. After the personal description the individual's fingerprint code appears, followed by relevant contact information should a police officer find him. On October 1, 1935, this bulletin became a national periodical, renamed the *FBI Law Enforcement Bulletin*.[20]

In the context of the immense popularity of tabloids and true crime magazines during the 1930s, Bureau publications were telegraphic and decidedly dry. The *New York Daily News* provides a good index of the growing popularity of tabloid crime coverage. When the paper began in 1920, it devoted only 6 percent of its space to crime coverage, but by 1930 23 percent of its space was given to crimes. The paper's circulation peaked in 1948, with a readership of five million (Buckland and Evans 16). True crime magazines also came into vogue during the 1930s and 1940s. According to Will Straw, "true crime magazines catered to public fascination with police procedures even as they recognized that police themselves were of little visual interest" (7). In true crime magazines the visual conventions of police sobriety and modern efficiency served as shorthand for police work and provided a gendered contrast to the provocative, full-color illustrations of women on the verge of being victimized that were featured on the covers of these magazines and repeated on the pages inside. Even as Hoover was busy overseeing the development of the exclusive look of Bureau publications, true crime magazines irreverently mimicked "authoritative ways of presenting information: mugshots, fingerprints, microscopic images, crime scene diagrams, maps and other genres of forensic imagery" (Straw 6). In effect, the zero-degree style of the Bureau's instrumental realism took on a second layer of meaning for popular audiences, which read the masculine sobriety of police work as sexy.

True crime magazines were popular in part because they fed the American public's growing fascination with police procedure and delivered on the public's ongoing interest in crime and punishment. While police photos of murder and execution were increasingly off-limits to the public, morbid images of crime and punishment continued to circulate in the tabloids and other unofficial arenas of image collection and display.[21]

In addition to its police bulletins, the Bureau continued to make and circulate public notices. While identification orders were primarily meant for the eyes of law enforcement officials, wanted flyers and placards were addressed to the American public at large and regularly distributed to more neutral locales such as post offices, in addition to being posted at police stations. In comparison to the titillating images offered up in true crime magazines and the tabloids, Hoover cultivated a dry, masculinized public address that matched the tone of Bureau documents circulated internally. In this manner he attempted to appeal to the public's sense of duty as a collection of respectable citizens, rather than to their questionable tastes as a "low" literary market fascinated by crime and police procedure.

The Ten Most Wanted

Hoover's resistance to the American public's popular fascination with crime began to erode with the establishment of the Most Wanted Program, born out of a cooperative venture between the FBI and the *Washington Daily News*. On February 7, 1949, an article entitled "FBI's Most Wanted Fugitives Named" appeared in the *Washington Daily News*. A reporter from United Press International had initiated this article by soliciting information from the Bureau, asking the FBI for the names and descriptions of the "toughest guys" it wanted to capture. According to an FBI publication commemorating the fiftieth anniversary of the "Top Ten Most Wanted" program, the FBI then published the names and photographs of the ten fugitives whom the organization considered "the most potentially dangerous" (Dove and Maynard 3). As the FBI tells it, the story generated so much publicity and was so appealing to the public that Hoover started the "Ten Most Wanted Fugitives" program the next year, on March 14, 1950 (Dove and Maynard 3).

Although the Bureau thus gave in to public tastes, it continued to stress the instrumental function of the program as a means of criminal identification and capture. According to the FBI, the program "worked": nine of the first twenty "Top Tenners" were caught due to citizen cooperation (Dove and Maynard 3). Following the general introduction of the Most Wanted Program, the FBI's fiftieth-anniversary commemorative publication describes the first "top ten" list in detail, offering short versions of each wanted man's story and capture and providing photographs of each of the men included in the first top ten. Overall this commemorative publication strikes one as a celebration of what is characterized as the happy, cooperative relationship between the FBI and the American public. The FBI thus commemorates not only itself but also, and more importantly, its partnership with the public.

Near the end of this book, the FBI supplies quotes from "Top Tenners" at capture—trite expressions of wacky encounters between criminals and the FBI at the moment of contact: "I'm glad it's over. I'm tired of running"; "Don't Shoot! Don't Shoot!"; "I was expecting you yesterday." Each feels familiar, as though it has been reproduced before, perhaps in a comic book or a classic Hollywood film. This series of quotes—yet another list—demonstrates the FBI's good-natured sense of humor about its superiority over the criminal element of society and, more important, its willingness to let the American public in on the joke.

In addition to the Most Wanted Program's clear instrumental function, it performs other work for the FBI. While it is not exactly "edutainment," this program might certainly be described as a sacrifice of information, given over to the public to appease them and garner their support. Ranking overtly signifies the Bureau's control over the information it keeps and attests to its expertise. By releasing this list to the public, then, the FBI lets the public in on a secret, but only so far. The exaggerated nature of the crimes advertised justifies the expanding power of the federal police, while also diverting attention away from the more mundane clerical work of the

Bureau. The FBI features spectacular criminals, thereby creating an association in the public imaginary between federal police work and heinous crimes. As a result, it conjures up an image of the FBI as focused on public defense against extreme criminal violence, rather than everyday acts of information collection and organization.

Within a decade of the introduction of the Most Wanted Program, the FBI was busy compiling extensive dossiers on Civil Rights leaders and other political activists. During the 1960s the FBI developed its Counter Intelligence Program, which targeted political dissidents and leaders of social movements for intensive domestic surveillance (including around-the-clock wiretapping) and reserved its most repressive tactics for African Americans and other people of color (Stabile, *Conspiracy* 267).

At the same time that the FBI was covertly engaged in the criminalization of dissent, it began issuing routine, but nonetheless spectacular, reports to the media stating that violent crime was increasing dramatically in the United States. Indeed, since the FBI first began issuing *Uniform Crime Reports* in 1932, these reports have uniformly demonstrated that crime in the United States is on the rise.[22] This fact is perhaps not too surprising, given that the FBI's funding is dependent upon the organization's ability to demonstrate steady or increased criminal activity in the United States. According to Carol Stabile, *Uniform Crime Reports* was usually released to the public "without much fanfare": "But beginning in September 1968, J. Edgar Hoover himself began to make monthly official pronouncements about dramatic increases in crime rates throughout the county, his presence ensuring intensified media coverage." According to Stabile, these appearances continued throughout the fall and promptly ended with the presidential election of Richard M. Nixon in November of 1968 (*Conspiracy* 271).[23]

It was from this context that law-and-order news of one crime wave after another emerged in the late 1960s.[24] The wave metaphor obscured the historical and contextual factors that made crime more likely. The temporal logic of the crime wave reflected postwar technologies of fear, which were increasingly structured by the everyday cycles of the commercial news media and aimed at the periodic production and reproduction of low-level fear, or what Brian Massumi aptly terms "ambient fear" (viii). Ambient fear, in turn, elicited vigilante viewers as model law-and-order citizens, who paid attention to the mugs paraded on the evening news. The premiere of *America's Most Wanted* in 1988 would consolidate these same viewers into an active audience of armchair crime fighters. As this program blurred police sobriety and tabloid journalism, viewers responded by learning to shift among the affective registers of titillation, fear, and moral indignation.

CHAPTER FIVE

America's Most Wanted

STILL ON THE AIR AFTER TWENTY YEARS, *America's Most Wanted* (AMW) is one of the longest-running programs in television history.[1] The weekly, hour-long program is coproduced by the FBI's Public Affairs Office and a regular production team at the Fox Network. While the program bills itself as a clearinghouse for wanted fugitives, its magazine format accommodates a variety of programming content, including profiles of wanted fugitives and missing children, highly stylized melodramatic reenactments of violent crimes, tips on how the home viewer can make his or her family less vulnerable to violent crime, vignettes on captured fugitives and recovered children, and sentimental video portraits of heroic law enforcement officials killed or maimed "in the line of duty."[2]

One of the first reality television programs ever produced,[3] *AMW* was also the first Fox program to surpass the shows counterprogrammed by the big three networks in terms of viewer ratings.[4] *America's Most Wanted* makes money for the Fox Network by making viewers feel like active participants in an ongoing series of manhunts. As host John Walsh told viewers in the premiere episode of *AMW*, the program marshals the communicative powers of television for the work of crime fighting: "Good evening from Washington, D.C. I'm John Walsh. Welcome to the premiere of *America's Most Wanted,* a weekly, nationwide criminal manhunt—a partnership with law enforcement agencies across the country." In the semantic shift from the "FBI's" to "America's" Most Wanted, the home viewer is promoted to the status of "partner" to the police. Reflecting this newly formed partnership, the program expects a friendly, supportive, and celebratory attitude toward police work from its viewers.

Televisual Community Policing

America's Most Wanted preps viewers for the work of crime fighting by repeatedly bringing the threat of violent crime home to them. One way the program achieves this is through dramatic reenactments of fugitive escapes and prison breaks. In these regularly featured segments *AMW* uses camera techniques to re-create the *Hands Up* effect exploited by Pinkerton's one century earlier. The television camera takes up the position of the police officers or prison guards whose lives are threatened by the dangerously out-of-control criminal. This device was used in the first reenactment featured on *AMW,* which opens by recounting the prison escape of David James Roberts. The viewer learns from the reenactment that Roberts tricked his guards into cuffing his hands in front of his body and loosening them so that he could eat a Wendy's hamburger. At the point in the story when the former prisoner takes control of his guards, the vocal track slows down until the fugitive sounds like a monster. The fugitive, played by an African American actor, looks menacing and points two shaky guns directly at the camera as he maniacally hollers something incomprehensible at his guards (home viewers). Walsh narrates the scene in voice-over: "In an instant, a nightmare, the guards became his prisoners, were forced to hand over their uniforms, which he would later use as a disguise." This premiere dramatic sequence was answered the following week with the astonishing report of Roberts's actual capture, "thanks to tips phoned in by home viewers."

It is perhaps not surprising, then, that viewer desire to participate in crime fighting through the medium of television quickly exceeded the program's instrumental function: to catch the particular fugitives it displayed in a given episode. In the show's first year on the air, it received five hundred calls per episode. By 1994 that number had risen to three thousand calls per show. But according to Pamela Donovan, very few of these calls led to arrests. As Donovan notes, this disparity between the number of calls and the amount of useful information gleaned suggests that "the desire to 'get involved'" was "considerably more widespread than those who may have come in contact with the criminal in question" (125). Indeed, *America's Most Wanted* emerged in the context of the effective dismantling of the welfare state and the rise of the law-and-order approach to social problems in the 1980s and 1990s.[5] At a time when Americans were feeling increasingly threatened, despite constant or declining crime rates, *AMW* answered to popular fantasies of a return to community policing.[6]

America's Most Wanted initially partnered with Crime Stoppers, an organization "based on the principal that 'Someone other than the criminal has information that can solve a crime' and . . . created to combat the three major problems faced by law enforcement in generating that information: Fear of REPRISAL, An attitude of APATHY, Reluctance to get INVOLVED."[7] Not long after Crime Stoppers chapters began cropping up across the United States, the National Crime Prevention Council (NCPC) was formed, broadcasting persuasive messages calling for a return to community policing in America.[8] The NCPC, which sponsors programs like Neighborhood Crime Watch, is perhaps best-known for its friendly mascot, McGruff the crime dog, who began to appear in public service announcements in 1980, urging adults and children alike to "take a bite out of crime." The NCPC attributes its historical emergence to a widespread sense of helplessness at the thought that only the police can fight crime. The origin story told by the NCPC on its Web site adopts the language of empowerment to describe its role in the lives of ordinary American citizens: "Thirty years ago people felt powerless, believing that only law enforcement officers could fight crime. Parks, street corners—and even schoolyards—were havens for criminals. But the leaders of 19 organizations decided enough was enough and worked together to develop the National Citizens' Crime Prevention Campaign." While citizen-policing programs bill themselves as "community" or "neighborhood" organizations, they in fact operate in a highly privatized and privatizing manner. Their members' ultimate concern is the protection of their homes and private property, which extends most profoundly, insistently, and with the largest doses of moral righteousness, to their children. The language used by the NCPC to describe the perceived threat of crime in the early 1980s reflects increasing moral panic about child safety. The figure of the missing or vulnerable child is already present in the NCPC's list of the imaginary locales of violent crime: "parks, street corners—and even schoolyards."[9]

America under Siege

Earnest viewers of *America's Most Wanted* belong to an imagined moral community united by fear and outrage and practice citizenship by policing their fellow citizens from the couch. Because it presents itself as a national clearinghouse, *AMW* produces a wildly exaggerated sense of the frequency and ferocity of violent crime in America. The show's gritty worldview is communicated most potently through its title sequence, which expresses a dire sense of emergency: America is under siege! Edited in a frenetic montage style and set to adrenaline-pumping music, the title sequence attempts to stimulate fear in home viewers. The original title sequence opens with an extreme close-up of a blinking eyeball. The eye looks off to one side (as if in fear). There is complete silence. Then a phone rings, and a woman's voice says, "I've been shot." The show's theme music kicks in, up-tempo 1980s synthesizer music that sounds like it might have come off of the *Beverly Hills Cop* soundtrack. A man's voice says, "Can you give me the information, ma'am?" Following is a sound effect of someone dialing a number. Another male voice answers the call: "Crimestoppers." Then a second woman's voice, terrified, is heard: "I have a real emergency." Cue sirens. A nondescript voice says, "Someone just got kidnapped." A woman's voice responds, "You stay on the line with me, okay?"

As this sequence of sound clips and effects unfolds, the viewer is confronted with interspersed shots of guns, police lights at night, recording equipment, police cars on the streets, SWAT teams preparing to rush a suspect, police dogs, silhouettes of men in a lineup, a baby's hand on a crib bar, a handcuffed man being escorted by two police officers, an empty tire swing moving in slow motion, a woman's face peeking through a chained front door out into the darkness, and handcuffs abandoned as though someone had just escaped from custody. The opening montage comes to an end with a big, booming sound effect, the *America's Most Wanted* logo growing large on the screen, along with the sound, and then disappearing.[10] The title sequence communicates a sense of emergency, and Walsh proposes citizen-police cooperation in matters of criminal identification as the solution.

AMW manages the fear and moral anxiety it stirs up by incorporating material that signifies citizen empowerment through crime fighting. The program regularly incorporates self-congratulatory stories of capture and repeatedly makes a point of thanking viewers for their help. Walsh, law enforcement officials, and victims and their family members openly express gratitude for the program's existence and the audience of caring, involved citizens watching from home. The gratitude expressed "signals" the viewer's membership in an empowered, if imagined, community (Cavender 91). "America" may be under siege, but *"America" Fights Back*—a phrase that was officially incorporated as the show's subtitle in the early 1990s.

America's Most Wanted's production and management of fear through the twin tropes of "America under siege" and "America fights back" reached a climax in a title sequence that aired in the fall of 1993 (Episode 295). This new sequence is no longer merely stimulating; it is excessive to the point of being overwhelming. With the proliferation of images included in the sequence, *AMW* reveals which bodies are perceived to be under threat and which bodies are considered menacing. The concrete embodiment of victim and perpetrator across the montage reveals that the empowerment promised by *America's Most Wanted* is specifically white empowerment. While the outlaws featured are a mix of Caucasians and African Americans, the African American outlaws are portrayed as the most dangerous. Several of the white outlaws featured are coded as "old" and/or "classic," in a manner that produces outlaw romance and nostalgia in the absence of an immediate threat. The victims portrayed in the title sequence are uniformly white women and children.[11] As Gray Cavender argues, "crime is a symbolic threat on *America's Most Wanted*," and the program ritually resolves this threat through displays of successful capture and arrest (84). But *AMW* communicates the symbolic threat of crime and its resolution via concrete embodiment by the particular individuals whom the program chooses to highlight.

Over the course of the show's extended run, the title sequence shrunk, prefaced by a congratulatory criminal count that extends to home viewers. This shift can be seen as early as Episode 163. Rather than opening with the title sequence, the show begins with a quick, scrolling sequence of mug shots, some images from the old title sequence, lineups, extreme close-ups of mug shots, and parts of faces rendered to look like silk screens. The mug shots dominate, flashing one after another as though in a Rolodex file. They go by so quickly that the viewer cannot absorb their contents, only the repetition of the form, which signals to the viewer that these are pictures of outlaws. There is an ominous, ambient low bass sound as the pictures flash across the screen. The male announcer's deep booming voice comes in: "To date your anonymous phone tips have led to the capture of 148 of America's Most Wanted."[12] A graphic of gold, shadowed numbers runs very quickly from 1 up to 148 over the scrolling faces of outlaws. This visual is paired with a "tick, tick, tick, tick" sound effect, as though the viewer is hearing the numbers mechanically click into place in quick succession. There is a careful accounting of those who got away versus those who served their time, the show attempting to move as many individuals as possible from one side of the balance sheet to the other. By the mid-1990s the show had dropped the title sequence altogether in favor of the criminal count (Episode 378). From then on the program has led with a message of viewer empowerment, which serves to frame and somewhat contain the program's fear-mongering segments.[13]

America's Most Wanted promises viewers narrative closure—specifically, criminal punishment as payoff for the suffering endured by the victims of violent crime. In the universe created by *AMW*, catching the fugitive is "the first step towards healing" for his victim(s). In vignettes about successful captures *AMW* routinely invites home viewers to imagine that they provided the definitive clue—to imagine, for instance, that the fugitive might have been spotted at the McDonald's in their hometown. In one episode viewers are in fact asked to celebrate the capture of one of *America's Most Wanted* "under the golden arches," of all places. Cut to an interview with a McDonald's manager, wearing a uniform and a headset, standing behind the counter: "He came in and ordered a cheeseburger, a fry, and a medium drink. I put a cheeseburger in the bag, walked around the fry station [the manager reenacts what he did as he tells the story], and I went back there and called the police. I knew the guy from like fifteen years ago when I was . . . you know I went to school with him and I was in the Cub Scouts with him" (Episode 190).

Headquarters

Each night John Walsh greets his viewers from the nation's capitol: "Hello from Washington, I'm John Walsh"—as though Walsh works for the FBI, not Fox. Through this elision the show claims to be purely interested in providing a public service, presenting itself as "real" and, therefore, more than mere entertainment. "Typically," writes Barbara A. Pitman, "this means the communication of some kind of information that viewers need to (or ought to) know about *as* the public" (172). The public consolidated by *AMW* is decidedly pro–law and order, a political position that is created, in part, through overt appeals to national belonging. By the fall of 1990 *AMW*'s logo was ferociously nationalistic, featuring a gold eagle in profile with talons outstretched as if ready to land on or pick up prey (Episode 139).[14] A gold circle rims the eagle image. Inside the gold circle is a gray circle with stars. Coming in from the right of the screen is the show's rectangular, gold-plated, engraved-looking logo: "AMERICA'S MOST WANTED." "America's Most" is stacked atop "Wanted," which is the graphic's most prominent element. As the logo locks into place, the show's musical theme fades out, and the screen behind the logo goes completely black.

On *AMW* the nation's capitol has become a Fox studio set where actors portray a strange mix of busy, caring volunteers working the phones and competent federal law enforcement personnel moving files around. From the program's inception the studio set has presented a mix of televisual sets with which the home viewer would already be familiar. It mimics a telethon set, with visible phone banks "manned" by volunteers. It prominently displays "new" communications technologies, not dissimilar to network news programming. And it is dressed to look like a detective's office, according to the conventions of film noir and televised crime dramas. Anna Williams notes the tension between the show's visual signs of police sobriety and its reliance upon the conventions of fictional genres: "While the show's location in Washington, D.C., invokes crime and law enforcement as national policy issues, the studio's mise-en-scène draws on specific generic conventions from television and movies" (99). In this manner *AMW* intentionally conflates the discourses of police sobriety with crime drama's promise of vicarious violence.

America's Most Wanted sticks to this basic formula for dressing the set, but it continues to grow more elaborate in terms of technological displays and the number and quality of actors on the set. Over the course of the show's run, it has come to look gradually less like a television news set and more like a police precinct or what the viewer might imagine a big, open shared office at the FBI looks like (Episode 163). In addition to the persons working the phones, there are desks, dressed up with "antique" desk lamps, where professional-looking men sit in suits and study papers. Women and men work the phones. Walsh stands among these "professionals," and when the cameras roll, he begins to walk out from the busy group and toward the camera. His mark keeps the other members of the *AMW* staff in frame behind him as he delivers the show's introduction. The program's mise-en-scène creates the impression that Walsh is the head of a big, powerful, hardworking organization, making the visual suggestion that these folks are working around the clock to help *you* keep America's streets clean.

On the set of *America's Most Wanted,* technological displays communicate the program's "logic of immediacy," or its up-to-the-minute access to information the public needs in order to fight crime in their own communities. By prominently featuring "state-of-the-art" communications technologies, the program attempts to frame itself purely in terms of its instrumental and pedagogical functions, as though entertainment and, therefore, advertising dollars were not also at stake (Pitman 173). By the late 1990s the technological exhibits had become even more elaborate. The number and size of the television monitors featured behind Walsh had increased, encouraging a flitting gaze from the home viewer. Consider the opening segment of a special program on sexual assault aired in the spring of 1998 (Episode 490). Walsh is centered in front of a wall of televisions playing different videos. One shows the capitol lit up against the D.C. night sky. Three are devoted to wanted posters or mug shots. One features a missing notice. Other screens feature random surveillance footage and other nondescript videos. The whole set is reminiscent of the technologically overloaded feel of a Nam June Paik sculpture, seeming to say: *Technology. We have it, lots of it.*

Behind Walsh actors "work" in a NASA-style arrangement at an elongated conference table, positioned at ground level and dwarfed by the walls of technology that surround them. Those sitting on the near side of the table face the home viewer and talk on telephones. Those sitting on the far side of the table face the television monitors and look from the screens on the wall to the computer screens positioned at their workstations, the telephones and television monitors prominently displayed on the set signaling interactivity.[15] Walsh steps away from the conference table and walks toward the camera: "Good evening. April is Sexual Assault Awareness month. . . . We start tonight with our latest on one of our most notorious rapists. A man whose been terrorizing NYC for years. . . . This animal has hunted and raped fourteen women, who live in buildings without doormen. All of his victims are young, attractive, and slender, and all have felt sheer terror at the rapist's demands" (cut to footage of the victims shot in silhouette). Here *AMW*'s show of access to technology authorizes the program's claims and worldview, even as it appears to create a direct, and possibly reassuring, line of communication between the program and its home viewers.

Head Crime Fighter

While *AMW*'s title sequence may titillate, and its opening teasers aim to make the viewer's heart race, Walsh sets a serious, professional tone. He embodies police sobriety, as do the law enforcement representatives featured on the show. The program's emotionalism comes through in the interviews with the victims; the dramatic reenactments; and Walsh's brief, calculated slips from sober host to morally outraged citizen. The address employed by *America's Most Wanted* is no longer exclusively the sober technocratic address of a J. Edgar Hoover, but the populist address of the Ad Council: If there's one thing we can all agree on, it is fear of violent crime and, more specifically, of someone breaking into our homes in the middle of the night to victimize us, or worse, our children.[16]

The show's sense of place, of taking the viewer "there," is crucial to the effective creation of an imaginary link between the home viewer and violent crime. The studio is in the nation's capitol—"headquarters"—but Walsh is routinely seen on location in various cities and towns across the United States. This demonstrates the show's ability to move the viewer from the local to the national and back again.[17] As the program skips across the country and across the faces of wanted fugitives, it gives the impression that all of this classified information and vast American geography are at the viewer's command—or rather, at Walsh's. He is the viewer's connection to the bigwigs: the FBI, the U.S. marshals, and the Postal Service. The viewer is invited along for the ride, but this is not just fun and games. This is serious, deadly serious.

Walsh models the appropriate demeanor for viewers. He is a tough citizen-cop, and he is a family man whose son was victimized by violent crime. The gendered dynamic established between Walsh and the viewers is powerful. He plays the substitute husband and father to America's victims, while the majority of victims featured on the show are women and children. In the vein of Uncle Sam, Walsh's signature gesture over the course of the series is pointing directly at the camera as he implores viewers: "We need *your* help. If *you* know anything, anything at all, please call our hotline at 1-800-CRIMETV."

Walsh's gendering of law enforcement as paternalistic comes through most powerfully in his costuming and body language. In the studio he's dressed like a detective: shirt, tie, and slacks. When on location he often wears a black leather jacket or a brown bomber jacket and jeans. Sometimes on location he sports a fitted white polo shirt and jeans. It is difficult to miss how conventionally handsome Walsh is, especially in the early episodes. He looks like an actor who might play a detective on a prime-time crime drama.

An early episode establishes this paternalistic dynamic between Walsh and the home viewer (Episode 18). Walsh is sitting on a desk on the right side of screen, a large television set positioned next to him on the desk, displaying the show's logo. The set behind the desk looks like a police station or a post office waiting room. There are accordion files and loose files casually arranged on a bookshelf and a bulletin board with wanted posters attached to it. Walsh is literally head and shoulders above the mug shot of the fugitive displayed on the television screen to his left, this arrangement creating a diagonal sight line from Walsh to the fugitive and back, extending into the upper right-hand corner of the screen, where the viewer can make out another set of mugs on a wanted poster hanging on the back wall. Dressed in this manner, the set establishes levels and layers of information and invites visual comparisons.

Walsh sits above the camera. A low-angle shot creates the impression that the home viewer is seated below Walsh, facing the desk. Walsh's posture and blocking suggest that he is about to lecture the home viewer, but in a nice way:

> Good evening, it's Sunday June 5th, and I'm John Walsh. One of the FBI's Ten Most Wanted fugitives has been captured near Palm Beach, West Florida. Accused racketeer John Darryl Farmer, wanted for a variety of crimes including two murders, is in custody tonight. *Your* phone calls made the difference. We'll have that story later in our program. But first the U.S. Marshals want *your* help in capturing one of their fifteen most wanted fugitives. His name is Norman Ray Freemont. Nearly two years ago Freemont was sentenced for a bank robbery in Vancouver. But he broke out of a supposedly escape-proof jail. And that's where we pick up his story.

As Walsh delivers this monologue, the fugitive's image appears on the television screen next to Walsh. A moment later the word "captured" appears over the fugitive's face. As Walsh tells viewers, "*Your* phone calls made the difference," the show cuts away from the low-angle shot to a second camera, which places the viewer almost level with the host. Walsh looks at the second camera with his head slightly down and a stern, yet encouraging expression on his face. Once Walsh has finished congratulating the show's vigilante viewers on the successful capture of Farmer, the show cuts back to the earlier, low-angle shot, which places the viewer beneath the host once again. As Walsh informs viewers about the next fugitive, two mug shots appear on the television screen to his left in quick succession: a profile shot followed by a frontal mug shot. If viewers want to get back on Walsh's level, they will have to call the hotline.

The tough love appropriate to the law-and-order approach to social problems comes through most clearly in special episodes of *AMW*, where Walsh takes on a particular issue pertinent to violent crime or law enforcement. In special episodes Walsh reluctantly exposes the viewer to the nastiness of the world: "Good evening from Washington, it's Friday, May 3rd, and I'm John Walsh. Tonight we target gang violence. Prosecuters say it's spreading like a plague. Street gangs are turning our neighborhoods into battlefields, our teenagers into drug addicts, and our children into moving targets" (Episode 163). Walsh walks toward the camera: "Nobody can argue this fact [points at viewer with pen]. Street gangs are selfish [point], brutal [point], and vicious [point]. They don't care who they hurt, you or your child." Walsh stops once, framed in a medium close-up shot. He stands still, his body language communicating to the viewer that he doesn't want to tell her this, but he has to. It is his duty. No matter how difficult it may be to hear, it is better that the viewer know the truth, admit the truth, and not try to argue against how vicious the world really is.

Victims' Rights

AMW marks a significant shift in the history of outlaw display, insofar as it signals its privatization, its entrance into the home. Of course, outlaw displays had previously entered American homes via newspapers, the *Police Gazette*, tabloids, true crime magazines, and television newscasts. However, *AMW* constitutes a significant break from these earlier displays, stressing its instrumental function and its status as a public service. This makes *AMW* more like an FBI wanted poster than an issue of the *Police Gazette* or the journalistic convention of televising a suspect's mug shot on the evening news.

America's Most Wanted electronically projects fugitives into the actual and imaginary space of the family home. As a result, the threat of stranger violence becomes undifferentiated from crimes against property. The program repeatedly underscores the difference between public and private space, coding these spheres in terms of race, class, and gender. According to Anna Williams, "the white middle class family functions as the privileged representative of the threatened population" addressed by *AMW* (99). Williams notes that the program defines crime exclusively in terms of violent crime, "the majority of whose victims are women and children" (99). As the imaginary locus of danger moves from the city and rural areas to the suburbs, fear of crime stimulates consumption and rationalizes segregated living environments. *AMW* deputizes ordinary home viewers to become suburban, as well as rural and urban, vigilantes. It is possible that the show in fact helped to produce the architectures of fear that proliferated during the 1980s and 1990s, such as gated communities and the revanchist city.

The privatization of outlaw reading practices was not merely a product of the form's migration to the medium of television. It also reflected the conservative embrace of the victim in the late 1980s and 1990s and the subsequent rise of the victims' rights movement in the United States.[18] As John Walsh declares in the show's very first episode, "We believe these stories demand telling." And, he might have added, deserve a hearing. *America's Most Wanted* contextualizes fugitive displays with victims' stories of violation. In so doing, it demands a relatively new practice of televisual witnessing not unrelated to the conventions of daytime television talk. Viewers of *AMW* are asked to witness not only outlaw displays and promises of punishment but also the suffering and outrage experienced by victims (Donovan 119). The program is, therefore, a novel hybrid of masculine and feminine addresses.

Walsh was chosen to host *AMW* in part because he was already a highly recognizable victim of violent crime. In response to his son's kidnapping and murder, Walsh had founded the National Center for Missing and Exploited Children (Donovan 126). His son's case had received a great deal of media attention and generated two made-for-television movies about the family's tragedy: *Adam* and *Adam: His Song Continues.* Incidentally, the actor Daniel Travanti played Walsh's character (Williams 113). Travanti was highly recognizable as one of the stars of *Hill Street Blues*—a popular 1980s crime drama that Todd Gitlin describes as "the first post-liberal cop show" (308; quoted in Fishman and Cavender 6). According to Gitlin, *Hill Street Blues* naturalized human suffering and reinforced the notion that institutions can do little to change this reality; at best, they can maintain a modicum of order (308). *America's Most Wanted* offers a vigilante's response to this state of affairs, purporting that Americans can in fact do something about violent crime.

While *AMW* incorporates women's and children's narratives of victimization and often provides women and children with opportunities to talk about their experiences on camera, their stories are consistently framed by men—predominantly by Walsh and by the show's male announcer.[19] Male law enforcement officials are also routinely called upon to verify a particular woman's or child's claims. At the same time *AMW* actively "pitches" victims to home viewers—in the language used by the male host and announcer, the melodramatic reenactments of violent crimes, and the interviews with victims. Victims are routinely described using adjectives that connote wholesomeness and physical attractiveness: "beautiful, innocent, talented, friendly, hard-working, etc." (Donovan 127). In the reenactments cinematic and televisual shortcuts are employed to situate victims "within an idealizing tradition of domestic relationships" (Williams 101). So, for instance, a young white couple is shown in a courtship scenario. Or perhaps a woman is shown at home in the kitchen, tending to her children. The program thus routinely presents and narrates victims as "heroes" (Donovan 128).

To the show's credit, its dramatic reenactments of violent crimes often feature capable women and resistant children, but they uniformly conclude with the violent spectacle of their victimization. Williams argues that the "spectacle of affect" generated by the melodramatic reenactments, punctuated by tearful interviews with victims, attempts to produce empathic identification between viewers and victims, but the point-of-view shots employed in the reenactments are most often attributable to the aggressor (102). Donovan concurs that *AMW* regularly encourages the viewer's visual identification with the perpetrator, through point-of-view, hand-held, and horror film–inspired shots. In some vignettes the program goes so far as to incorporate the sound effect of heavy, interiorized breathing, as though the viewer occupies the predator's body (Donovan 129). Williams writes: "In contrast to the interviews with victims, the bodies of the women in these reenactments are eroticized in relation to their proximity to violence. They appeal to masculine fantasies about the humiliation, rape, and mutilation of women and children—fantasies about the imposition of absolute power on people culturally coded as property" (103–4). The notable exception to this rule occurs in reenactments of prisoner escapes, in which the camera takes up the position of the guards, thereby cultivating viewer identification with law enforcement. What remains consistent across these two very different types of reenactments is the cultivation of viewer identification with masculine agents of violence.

It is not only in the melodramatic reenactments that *America's Most Wanted* cultivates the sadistic or prurient consumption of images of brutalized women and children. In one episode, for example, the program is given over to a story about three girls who were molested by their step-father. "Tonight," the announcer intones, "you can give them a precious gift: justice" (Episode 278). Walsh, from the studio set, implores viewers to watch the segment: "Not too long ago, we got a letter from three sisters in Chicago. Tonight, I'm asking you to watch their story. It's a very different approach for us. There are no actors. These teenage girls speak very frankly about their sexual and physical abuse. It may not be appropriate for younger children to watch. And it'll be tough for adults to watch too. But these girls really need your help." Throughout the segment that follows viewers are consistently reminded that the teenage girls asked for their story to be covered by *AMW*. All three young women are white and conventionally attractive. The vignette features video footage of the sisters speaking casually with a correspondent; showing family photos; and detailing episodes of molestation, including one story of a "Christmas-morning ritual" in which the stepfather annually forced one of the young women to perform oral sex on him while their mother looked the other way.

Walsh's setup for the story expresses indignation, but the camera tells another story. A large portion of the interview takes place in a private pool, where the three young women swim, lounge, and discuss their sexual abuse in graphic detail. The camera lingers over their young bodies. It is as though *AMW*, and by extension the home viewer, has taken up the stepfather/molester's point of view. As they "break the silence," *AMW*'s cameras molest them all over again. Stressing the "teenage girls'" role as initiators (of the story), the segment leaves the viewer with the sense that it must have been their idea to appear in bathing suits as a sign of their empowerment. Perhaps it was their idea: inviting inappropriate sexual attention is one of the possible signs of sexual abuse.[20]

Firmly rooted in John Walsh's autobiography of victimization, *AMW* privatizes morality in a manner that allows the expressive violence of vernacular reward notices to reenter public discourse, only this time with a national address directed at a mass audience. The announcer's voice warns home viewers: "There's a predator in paradise. Among the sun and fun in Orlando, he's stalking *your* child." Cut to a recording of a nine-year-old victim of a child molester active in the Orlando, Florida, area. A male adult feeds the child leading questions: "You thought he was trying to put something in your mouth?" The child answers, "Yes." A local law enforcement agent expresses his desire to "put that sick freak away." *AMW* shares photos of the child molester and tells us that now he's out on house arrest, blaming a lenient judge and displaying her professional portrait for the home viewer's consideration. She is photographed in her robe, sitting on the bench, before an American flag.[21] Six months after his house arrest, *AMW* informs the viewer, the molester had removed his tracking device and escaped. Another law enforcement official opens up for the camera: "I can't tell you how angry I get . . . we had this dirt bag in our grasp . . . this low-life pedophile." At the conclusion of the segment, Walsh comforts viewers with the promise of relevant child-safety advice: "If you go on vacation with your kids this summer, we've got tips to help you stay safe. Please visit our safety center online" (Episode 944).

The personalized address employed by Walsh and other law enforcement officials in the Disney World story cultivates emotional identification with individual members of the victims' rights movement and, by extension, ideological affinity with the movement. Walsh or some cop working on a case is "man enough" to reveal his true feelings: "I can't tell you how angry I get." The program's posture of moral outrage is possible precisely because Walsh is a private citizen. When a law enforcement official shares his disgust with particular fugitives, the viewer is encouraged to consume said emotional displays as proof of the official's humanity. He is revealing himself to be a private individual with feelings. When crime is personalized in this manner, it requires viewers to exercise empathy with respect to the host, the program and its aims, and most especially with the victims.

As in the Disney segment, *AMW* often profiles criminals who committed their crimes while out on bail, parole, or house arrest. The program endorses stricter sentencing, higher bails, and the death penalty. The first two are explicitly endorsed by the show's host but presented as his personal opinions, therefore carrying the moral weight of his narrative of personal suffering. The show endorses the death penalty only indirectly, through the voices of particular enraged victims or members of their families. The Disney segment's work of political persuasion is further obscured by its conclusion, which gestures toward the show's status as a public service.

AMW frequently covers crime thematically and regularly accompanies reports with authoritative tips on how home viewers can keep from being victimized by violent crime. This communicates the program's masculine facility in moving the viewer from the specific to the general and back again. By offering tips to the home viewer, *AMW* resumes a direct address, thereby underscoring the threat it just communicated to the home viewer. In the same move the knowledge generated by the story is swiftly encapsulated into the frame of practical know-how in a tough world, shedding all traces of its function as a political response to the policies and procedures of the American criminal justice system. Significantly, *America's Most Wanted* never calls for violent retribution; it just claims that it wants to "lock 'em up and keep 'em there." "Let 'em rot in jail" is the show's ethos. However, the visual relationship cultivated between vigilante viewers and the criminals the program features is alternatively threatening toward the home viewer and sadistic toward both the victims featured in the reenactments and the real outlaws verbally disparaged by the show.

Missing and Exploited

John Walsh has used *America's Most Wanted* as a platform for his nonprofit organization, the National Center for Missing and Exploited Children. He has done as much if not more than any other individual to bring the missing child to prominence as an ideological figure of innocence in the American popular imagination.[22] Over the course of the show's run, *AMW* has increasingly split airtime between outlaw and victim displays. The program juxtaposes displays of guilt and innocence through the twin televisual frames of the missing notice and the wanted poster, visually distinguishable, if at all, only through slight changes in the coloration of the graphic templates used. With these two displays presented in exactly the same format, home viewers are invited to compare and contemplate the bodily differences between the physical descriptions of full-grown fugitives—six feet tall and two hundred pounds—and missing children—three feet tall and forty-five pounds. The striking difference in physical stature underscores child vulnerability and innocence, as viewers are invited to watch reenactments and imagine scenarios of violent physical confrontations between these two body types.

AMW famously mixes dramatic reenactments of crimes with documentary photographs and footage of criminals. The reenactments are highly formulaic, creating a tension between generic treatments of crime and the program's pride in sharing specific details. The pull between the generic and the specific incites home viewers to fantasize about violent crime in their own lives. This particular function of the program has become more acute over time. The program claims to cultivate an individualizing look in home viewers, who are repeatedly asked to take a closer look: "Have you seen *this* man?" Or, "Please call us if you think you may have seen *this* little girl. Her parents are anxious for some news." However, over the course of the series, because of faster editing and denser programming, the viewer has become unable to hold onto all of the details speeding past. What remains are the rough outlines, the formulaic narratives of good versus evil, of innocents victimized by bad guys.

While the program clearly serves an instrumental purpose and uses outlaw and victim displays in order to facilitate identification and capture or recovery, it also, and perhaps inadvertently, cultivates a classificatory look in the home viewer. Sharp contrasts, on the order of myth, are established between the outlaws and victims profiled on *AMW*. Cavender writes that *AMW*'s criminals are "recurring stereotypes, stand-ins for contemporary social concerns" (82). "Criminals," he writes, "are described in terms that connote physical ugliness. They are depicted as dangerous, depraved, unremorseful people" (82). Cavender notes further that "in contrast to their loathsome criminals, *AMW*'s . . . victims are depicted as respectable, often physically attractive people, e.g., 'a good-looking college kid' or 'a pretty young wife.' The victims, who typify innocence and beauty, shape our sense of the crime problem as dirty and threatening" (82).

AMW creates a worldview of "us versus them" through Walsh's repeated use of the pronoun "we" and the visual juxtaposition of victim and outlaw displays.[23] Consider a brief segment from a "special episode" on sexual assault. After a journalistic-style story about "the East Side Rapist," the program returns to the studio, where a police sketch of a generic-looking African American man is displayed on the largest of the television screens behind Walsh, just over his left shoulder. Over his right shoulder a smaller screen shows an elementary-school portrait of a white girl, captioned with the word "missing." The words "America fights back" appear over the generic black man's face. Walsh points at the camera: "So let's see if *we* can stop him tonight. The East Side Rapist is a light-skinned African American man." There is no getting around the visual comparisons invited in this segment between a generic African American assailant and a specific young white victim, even though in this case the East Side Rapists' victims were adult women, and the missing-child display has nothing to do with the sketchy criminal being profiled.

Another opportunity for slippage from the individual to the type occurs in the interplay between the program's dramatic reenactments and its televisual wanted posters. The actors hired by the show seldom resemble the fugitives whom they portray, although the casting does reflect the racial or ethnic identity of the fugitive. Thus, an African American actor will play an African American fugitive, and an Asian American actor will play an Asian American victim.[24] Given how faulty eyewitness testimony is, one wonders whether a significant percentage of the tips called into the show are based on perceived matches with the actor, rather than with the fugitive pictured in the televisual wanted poster at the end of the segment. Considering the fact that the program spends a lot more time on a particular reenactment than it does showing a specific wanted poster, it seems likely that the show would breed the visual confusion characteristic of racist practices of looking.

America's Most Wanted routinely displays missing white children to motivate viewers to fight crime from home. When one considers the media images of African American child victims in circulation during the early 1990s in media venues other than *AMW*, the show's victim displays appear all the more biased. Deborah McDowell notes that postmortems of African American boys and teenagers began to appear in major metropolitan newspapers and on the covers of news magazines "with stunning regularity in 1990" (154). These images featured homicide victims, rather than missing children, their likenesses exploited to represent inner-city violence, decay, and family breakdown—among other social ills—rather than the middle-class white family besieged by crime.[25]

"America" Fights Back

The "we" constituted by *America's Most Wanted* includes select victims of violent crime, law enforcement officials, and sympathetic home viewers. In addition to victim and outlaw displays, the program regularly features sentimental portraits of law enforcement officials. In one episode law enforcement officials act as the family of an unidentified child victim (Episode

163). Walsh introduces the story: "One last piece of news [camera on Walsh with phone banks behind him]. Two months ago deputies in Dane County, Wisconsin, found an unknown girl. She'd been beaten and stabbed to death. We showed you her picture. And we heard from hundreds of parents of missing kids. It was heartbreaking, but we still don't have a lead in this case. Take another close look at this girl, and see if you recognize her." Cut to a black-and-white photo of the white girl that fills the entire screen. It is an arresting moment, given the fast-paced editing of the rest of the program.

As the viewer contemplates the child's portrait, Walsh implores: "She's somebody's daughter, neighbor, or somebody's sister—people that are desperate to know where she is." Cut to a missing poster of the girl: "If you know her name or anything about her, call us at 1-800-CRIME91." *AMW* lingers on the portrait for a full four seconds and then for another six seconds on the missing notice, featuring the same photo, now framed and captioned. Walsh's voice-over continues: "For now, the Dane County Deputies have become her family. And this week in a touching ceremony, they buried her. Deputies were her pallbearers and said a few kind words. Dedicated cops with a heart."

AMW then runs a human-interest story that might also accurately be described as police propaganda. The viewer is invited to watch a montage of cops loading a casket into a hearse and the hearse driving through the cemetery. As these images roll, a cop's voice is heard: "Because no one has stepped forward, we are the family for this young woman. Two and a half months ago, she entered our lives. We don't know a lot about her, but this young victim represent [*sic*] all victims to us, that we are sworn to protect. May you rest in peace, for we shall not, as we continue to wrestle with this case." Cut to more footage of the funeral. One cop stands to address his fellow officers: "Let us use today to remind us of our duty to all victims: the duty to protect and serve." Cue someone performing "Amazing Grace" at the funeral, and cut to shots of the flowers on the casket. This is followed by shots of officers' kids and wives in attendance at the funeral. The segment ends with a cop delivering a Christian prayer, followed by more shots of male and female officers tearing up. "Amazing Grace" comes to an end, and the segment closes on a blurry, extreme close-up of funeral flowers. Cut to commercial.

Also included in the "we" addressed by *America's Most Wanted* are the show's corporate sponsors. In one episode aired in January of 1994 (Episode 300), John Walsh shows the home viewer a series of missing notices: "Please call us if you know anything about the disappearance of either of these girls. And remember: you can call us when a child goes missing or to report the sighting of one. That's what we're here for. We're here to help. In fact, last month, we asked you to help find James Pierce. Pierce is accused of abducting three-year-old Katy Dawson from an Indiana Walmart. Store employees quickly responded, and Katy was reunited with her mother. Tonight, James Pierce is behind bars." As Walsh delivers this monologue, the fugitive's picture flashes up in a split screen with Walsh. A red banner with white lettering appears under his picture: "Surrendered."

Cut to a video of the three-year-old in close-up, saying, "I want him in jail." The child's father explains: "She took the front page of the newspaper last night and said 'uh, that's James Pierce' [shot of newspaper], and we never told her that. She knows what the guy looks like and what he did. She goes, 'Daddy you ain't gonna let that man git me no more are you?' I go, 'No, that man, you don't have to worry about that man anymore.'" Cut to a close-up of Katy: "I hope he won't hurt my Mommy or me, or I'll whip his butt." Cut to shots of Katy playing with her mom. Walsh narrates in voice-over: "This is three-year-old Katy Dawson. Her playfulness is just returning after a Christmas her family will never forget. The day Belinda Dawson lost her daughter during a trip to Walmart." Cut to a shot of the storefront, the camera slowly zooming in, then to video of Katy's mother sitting with her at the piano, dressed with Christmas-carol sheet music. Katy's mom wears a Christmas sweater. "It happened in minutes," she says. "We were talking to each other, and next thing I knew I didn't hear Katy's voice. And then I started looking around the store and looking around the aisles and the toys and no Katy."

Shots of store aisles appear as Walsh narrates how Katy's mother informed employees that her daughter was missing. The employees, Walsh notes, didn't panic because they had already come up with a plan, just months before the incident: "They called it Code Adam. The inspiration for the plan was my son, Adam, who was abducted twelve years ago from a Florida shopping mall." As Walsh mentions his son, the segment cuts to a close-up on a baseball portrait of Adam, which fades into a school portrait of Katy. Walsh continues, "So when little Katy disappeared, the employees were ready."

Walsh describes the emergency plan: employees announced a description of the missing child over the PA system, locked all the doors to the store, and dropped what they were doing in order to search the store for the child. Viewers learn that Katy was spotted near a rear entrance with the strange man. An employee called out to her, "Excuse me, where are you going?" She turned around and said, "Could you take me to my mommy, please?" Cut to a shot of Katy's mom saying, "We were both crying."

Walsh continues with the story. "Now that he's in jail," he says, "Katy's mother says she feels more at ease." Cut to video of Katy singing "Amazing Grace." Then her father says, "It's a good thing that it did happen at Walmart because when Code Adam was released, he was automatically sealed from leaving the premises." Walsh tells viewers that because Code Adam "worked so well here, Walmart has decided to roll it out to all stores both nationally and internationally. This will affect roughly 500,000 associates so it will bring recognition to the problem and the solution and raise awareness nationwide of what to do in case this happens." Walsh ends the segment by telling the viewer that Pierce had been paroled three times before trying to kidnap Katy, then shares his final thoughts on the matter: "I don't believe Pierce ever should've been let out in the first place."

In another segment, aired in the fall of 1996 (Episode 422), John Walsh stands in front of the camera with two kids. The Caucasian boy on his right wears a tie and holds a plaque for heroism. Walsh, tightly holding the hand of the Asian American girl on his left, tells the story of how these children knew what to do in an emergency and helped save their parents' lives by calling 911. After relaying their tales of heroism, Walsh informs the viewer: "Now they knew what to do because they were prepared. Every August there's a program that will help *you* know what to do. It's one that *you* [wagging his finger] should know about." Cut to footage of kids holding placards and being videotaped in a Blockbuster store. An employee asks a child, "What's your name?" The child responds, "My name is . . ." Walsh explains what the viewer is watching in voice-over: "One day the video-tapes made here could bring home one of these children. With the help of the Blockbuster Kidprint Program, the faces, personalities and mannerisms of these children will be captured on tape—a valuable tool to use if any of these children disappear."

Cut to an interview with a mother who has brought her children in to be "printed": "It takes one split second for a child to disappear, and if I've got something that shows what my child looks like, that's contemporary, that shows his personality and his mannerisms, it gives the local police department and other agencies a leg up on trying to help me find my child." Cut to a shot of a man in fatigues holding a missing-child flier. In voice-over Walsh tells the viewer why videotapes are particularly helpful aids: "Police need current pictures when trying to find a missing child, but the most helpful tool is home video. Since 1990 Blockbuster has 'kidprinted' more than one million children. During that time even children have begun to learn the importance of having home video." Cut to footage of a "printed" kid: "If I get lost or someone kidnaps me, they know what my voice sounds like and they can find me."

Walsh tells the viewer that the Kidprint program is offered every August: "It's fast, friendly, and free." A Blockbuster representative chimes in: "It takes five minutes of your time to bring your child in. We'll ask 'em to step in front of the camera. It may be the most important video that you ever own." Cut to shots of kids happily submitting to "kidprinting." Walsh captions the video: "The kids seem to enjoy the experience. And any time you can get kids to have fun doing something good for them, then you know you've taken the right step." More footage of the store and various white, middle-class kids getting "printed" and "mugging" for the camera. At the end of the segment, the viewer returns to Walsh at the awards ceremony: "Programs like Blockbuster Kidprint are designed to bring kids home safely. The sad fact is, sometimes they don't work. There's really nothing you can do to make your child safe. That harsh reality hit us all here on *America's Most Wanted* on a story we've been following a couple of years. The disappearance of little Katy Poltan." *America's Most Wanted* cultivates a sense of community that Cavender aptly describes as "neighborliness grounded in religion." Evidence of Cavender's claim can be found in the program's airing of footage of religiously framed candlelit vigils and Christian funerals for victims; the recurrence of planned and spontaneous performances of "Amazing Grace"; and statements by the show's host, and in interviews with law enforcement personnel or family and friends, that "our prayers are with you." Given the Walmart and Blockbuster segments, I would add an additional modifier to Cavender's phrase: *AMW* cultivates corporate neighborliness grounded in religion.

America's Most Wanted implicitly condones a Christian worldview of reality as a battle between the forces of good and evil. In a "special episode" on terrorists, aired in 1993 (Episode 295), Walsh opens the program with the story of a missing child recovered just in time for "Christmas": "Good evening from Washington. I'm John Walsh and welcome to a special edition of *America's Most Wanted* as we join the manhunt for accused terrorists. But first, I'd like to bring you some great news from last week's show. You've reunited a seven-year-old boy with his family. In 1990 Brian was abducted from his aunt's home in New Jersey. For three long years his mother hoped and prayed for a miracle. Well, you've helped make her dreams come true, because just two hours after last week's broadcast, Brian was found." Cut to video of the mother and son's reunion at the airport. She is excited, nervous, hysterical, holding one of his old stuffed animals. She seems very aware of the cameras, and so does he. He's being a good boy. She runs hysterically over to him. He seems calm and perhaps in shock, not openly emotional. The scene feels choreographed for the camera. Walsh narrates the footage in voice-over: "After spending three years apart, Brian and his mom finally had a chance to get reacquainted. It took only a few moments before shock and confusion gave way to joy." Walsh offers this explanation for the son's apparent blankness, his visible lack of enthusiasm or recognition.

Walsh continues: "This reunion was the end of a mother's nightmare, which police say began when Maria Stuart divorced this man, Francis Hatmaker. Francis Hatmaker is legally Brian's stepfather. After the divorce he refused to give Brian up." As Walsh says *this man*, sinister music comes in, and the program cuts to a close-up of a black-and-white photo of a man wearing dark sunglasses. As Walsh continues to frame the story, a child portrait of Brian wipes onto the right half of screen, creating a split-screen effect, with Hatmaker on the left and Brian on the right. The split screen makes a visual statement about the mother's right to separate these two by divorcing Hatmaker and simultaneously dramatizes Hatmaker's insistence that they stay together, side by side, like their photos. The child portrait is in color, whereas the adult man appears in gritty black and white, with a mustache and dark glasses. The visual comparison is sinister. Walsh goes on: "Instead, police say, he decided to kidnap him. Thanks to you, authorities found Brian and Hatmaker living in a hotel in Phoenix, Arizona. Hatmaker was arrested and taken to the Maricopa county Jail." As Walsh shares this victory with home viewers, the program cuts away from the split screen to shots of Phoenix, the facade of the Maricopa Jail, and finally back to the airport-reunion video. Brian now holds his stuffed animal, smiles, and walks beside his mother. The boy smiles directly at the camera, and his mother cues him to perform for it: "Are you happy? What do you want to say?" He smiles obediently and shrugs. Walsh finishes the story: "He was charged with kidnapping, and Brian was heading for home."

The segment then cuts to a close-up of Brian on video, saying, "It's good to be home." Cut to a close-up of mom and boy holding hands. The shot pans out to show them walking together, hand in hand. Cut to a night shot of the extended family outside a private home. "Okay, are you all ready to have Christmas?" says Mom. Everyone laughs. "Okay, let's go." Walsh's voice-over kicks in again as we watch the family enter the house: "On Christmas 1990, after Brian was abducted, his family put up this tree. Each Christmas since then Brian's family has left gifts under the tree—a symbol of their hope and faith. Finally, Brian is home to open his presents." During the voice-over the program cuts to interior shots of a living room or family room with a fully decked-out Christmas tree. Brian's extended family surrounds the tree. Someone is videotaping the event. As Walsh speaks, the segment features a tighter shot of the tree and the mantelpiece. The camera pans down to children sitting under the tree, surrounded by presents, then cuts to a close-up of Brian's face looking down at a present in his lap. The camera pans out to reveal Brian opening a present with family members positioned closely around him.

The video then returns to a shot of the tree as Brian's mother tearfully exclaims: "The Christmas tree still stands, and Brian's home. We put it up like the statue of liberty, the free, and you're gonna come home, the tree was Brian's coming home." Brian's mom delivers this speech from the couch, where she sits with a male relative or partner. His arm is wrapped around her. He looks at her tenderly. The segment then cuts to a shot of Brian with his hands together, held up to his mouth as if in a prayer position. He looks joyous. "It's been a very good day," he says to the camera. He appears to be performing a racist stereotype of a "chinaman." Brian bows slightly and turns away from the camera. Everyone in his family laughs. His mom pulls him close for a hug. The *AMW* logo appears in the lower left-hand corner of screen. Fade to black, and cut to commercial.

This segment not only attests to what Cavender aptly describes as *AMW*'s "neighborliness grounded in religion." It also demonstrates the program's production and reproduction of what Eve Kosofsky Sedgwick calls "Christmas effects," where multiple ideologies momentarily click into eerie alignment: "The thing hasn't, finally, so much to do with propaganda for Christianity as with propaganda for Christmas itself. They all—religion, state, capital, ideology, domesticity, the discourses of power and legitimacy —line up with each other so neatly once a year, and the monolith so created is a thing one can come to view with unhappy eyes" (6). In this segment Christianity, patriotism, xenophobia, consumer sentimentality, possessive individualism, and family as a particular picture of white suburban whole-someness—all line up in a row, such that "It's good to be back home" means "It's good to be back home, where children are free to perform for their parents (and the camera) in exchange for presents, and the child-centered family is free to make and consume racist jokes without fear of reproach. God Bless America."

What is most remarkable about the "Home for Christmas" segment is its inclusion in a "special episode" on terrorism. The magazine format of *America's Most Wanted* makes the juxtaposition of a missing-child-recovery vignette with profiles of wanted terrorists seem utterly arbitrary, the two therefore disconnected. But the conservative embrace of the missing child in the 1980s and 1990s set the stage for the federal government's exploita-tion of both victim and outlaw displays in response to the terrorist attacks of September 11, 2001. In the stark moral and visual culture established by *America's Most Wanted,* the victim, rather than the outlaw, has become the mask for state-sponsored violence. It is her image, as much if not more than the outlaw's, that motivates the vigilante viewer's sentimental identification with the authorities.

CONCLUSION

The Vigilante Viewer Rides Again

ON SEPTEMBER 17, 2001, PRESIDENT GEORGE W. BUSH invoked the wanted poster's magic in a popular domain saturated with xenophobia and American imperialist nostalgia. His response was politically adept. If one considers the possibility that the real target on 9/11 was not the buildings or the people in them but a globally recognizable icon of capitalism, then the president's turn to a popular icon of the American frontier makes perfect sense.[1] What is more, Americans were genuinely angry and fearful. Many probably would have preferred the unorthodox methods of a ruthless, lone bounty hunter to the tragically misplaced efforts of the U.S. military. But as the histories of posting collected here reveal, one cannot gain the comfort of a nostalgic cultural form without the attendant pressures of the violent economic and political traditions that form has served in the actual American past.[2] By way of conclusion this chapter draws upon the historical practices enumerated in this book to analyze American visual cultures of crime and punishment since 9/11.

Chapter 1, "Execution Broadsides," documented the

active role once played by Americans in live scenes of violent punishment. Puritan spectators at a live execution were the coperformative witnesses of religiously framed punishments. As crime and punishment were slowly secularized over the course of the eighteenth and nineteenth centuries, moral concerns did not entirely vanish from scenes of crime and punishment but were realigned in the consumer of crime broadsides, where moralistic frames barely contained the sensationalism of the details offered for the reader's consideration. Under the George W. Bush Administration, the moralistic consumer achieved the status of model citizen. In a time of national crisis, Bush asked Americans to exercise good citizenship through practices of consumption, rather than sacrifice.[3] Recalling the nineteenth-century shift from the scene of punishment to the scene of the crime, Americans obsessed over and became tourists of Ground Zero at the expense of public attention to undisclosed scenes of punishment. With the "leak" of Saddam Hussein's execution video over the Internet, Americans were invited to view, if not attend, an execution once again.[4]

Chapter 2, "Slave Notices," tracked the development of purportedly neutral police technologies of representation and display out of the explicitly racist visual conventions of the anthropological mug shot. Before the mug shot's zero-degree style was used to render the criminal an object of police science, its shallow, frontal take was used as a pseudoscientific means of othering. The conventions of the mug shot were used to picture nonwhite persons, who were regularly treated and visualized according to what Ella Shohat and Robert Stam have called the "animalizing trope" of empire, or "the discursive figure by which the colonizing imaginary rendered the colonized beastlike and animalic" (19). This decidedly violent history of photography's service to empire is highly significant in the context of the U.S. government and military's neocolonialist production and circulation of "the faces of terror" after 9/11.

Of particular relevance to American visual cultures of crime and punishment after 9/11 is chapter 2's discussion of the return to vigilante violence in the South after the Civil War. The practice of lynching—its photographic documentation and mass circulation—was used to terrorize African Americans and attest to continued white supremacy. These scenes of torture emerged out of a postwar context of defeat, economic insecurity, and political upheaval. They were the products of feelings of powerlessness and frustration, mixed with the moral determination that someone must be punished. Considering the deep historical connections between the mug shot and the lynching postcard in American history, the coexistence of sober FBI posters for wanted terrorists and pornographic scenes of torture coming out of Abu Ghraib is no longer quite so shocking. The latter set of images are not so much racist interpretations of Christian Evangelical faith, but souvenirs of military service created by bored soldiers and private contractors with little oversight and no clear sense of purpose. White Americans mugging for the camera next to horrific scenes of brutalized nonwhite bodies invite comparisons to the earlier postcards.[5] Between the "faces of global terror" posters circulated by the State Department and the digital "postcards" sent from Abu Ghraib, we have access to the Janus-faced character of American visual cultures of crime and punishment—at once modern and premodern, civilized and primitive.

From the vantage point of the present, chapters 3 and 4, "Pinkerton Posters" and "The FBI's Most Wanted," may read like playbooks for the Bush Administration's visual rhetoric in the "war on terror." I discuss the connections at length in what follows, but for now I want to briefly signal some of the major points of comparison. The president's ritual invocation of the iconic wanted poster of the frontier imaginary in response to 9/11 allowed him to assume the role of the cowboy-as-American-hero. It also functioned to mask the violence of the state with the so-called primitive violence of terrorism. By adopting the language of war, as J. Edgar Hoover had before him, President George W. Bush played on the public's sense of emergency. Repeated references to the extreme nature of the events of 9/11 served as a rationale for unlimited violence by the state, increased domestic surveillance, and less transparency on the part of the federal government. Bin Laden's outrageous and horrific stardom seemed to elicit more and more extreme measures from the federal government and the U.S. military. The Bush Administration thus adopted a paranoid, authoritarian posture not unlike J. Edgar Hoover's and, like Hoover, showed no small amount of disdain in response to public requests for greater transparency in the administration of government and war.

Chapter 5, "America's Most Wanted," discussed the conservative embrace of the victim in the 1980s and 1990s. The visual culture of *America's Most Wanted* repeatedly displayed victims and outlaws in tandem for a period of twenty years. In the name of protecting victims' rights, the program repeatedly called for harsher sentencing, increased surveillance, and the necessity of crime-prevention training. Through the guise of access to information about crime and the televisual conceit of interactivity, the program regularly race-baited its audience and implicitly promised white empowerment. *America's Most Wanted* addressed citizens who felt under attack and confirmed that feeling by recourse to threats far removed from the material threats actually faced by the majority of its viewers. The stark moral universe of innocents and "perps" created by *AMW,* and the Fox Network's nonfictional programming more generally, set the stage for the Manichean worldview promulgated by the Bush Administration. In what follows, I explore vernacular and professional practices of fugitive display in response to the events of 9/11.

Missing

In the immediate aftermath of the terrorist attacks, some New Yorkers papered the city walls with missing posters for their lost loved ones. As a practical response to the failure of the city's infrastructure and communications technologies during and immediately after the crisis, the collective turn to these low-tech communication tools is not surprising. Flyers were a readily available means of expression, and they offered a quick and meaningful way to reclaim the shared space of the city. With so much leveled, the flyers aimed to set things upright again. They moved New Yorkers back to the vertical plane of walking, reading, and talking their way through the city. All told, some ninety thousand missing notices drew passersby into spontaneous acts of reading, mourning, and keeping vigil.[6]

The missing-person flyers have been theorized as portraits of grief that briefly inhabited the border between the missing and the dead.[7] In the missing posters uncertainty was expressed not through the photograph per se, but through the relationship between image and text. What pricked readers was the combination of an ordinary family snapshot and the label: "missing." The reassuring presence offered up in the snapshot coexisted with the notification that the person pictured was absent. As the days dragged on, what had initially been desperate yet hopeful communication

New York City, September 11, 2001.
(Courtesy New York Historical Society; photograph
by Joseph Rodriguez/Gallery Stock)

tools for finding lost loved ones became raw expressions of grief. Nancy
Miller notes that the *New York Times* marked this shift in its second day of
reporting by changing the title of its series "Among the Missing" to "Portraits of Grief" (113).[8]

As time passed and the missing posters lost their instrumental function,
the abrupt and naive character of these texts took on greater cultural significance. The flyers came to seem like so many perfectly brilliant, intuitive
responses to the attacks, which appeared to viewers (especially those who
watched from a distance) in the visual codes of Hollywood special effects.
For those who watched the crisis unfold on television, the neighborhood
aesthetic of the missing notice offered a poignant alternative to the global
media barrage of hyperreal, full-color moving images of catastrophe. Fabricated in the midst of what seemed total and overwhelming destruction, the
scrapbook quality of the flyers was visual proof of action in the face of chaos
and grief, thereby communicating the possibility that even this horror

Image from the *Here Is New York* Collection, New York, 2001.
(Courtesy New York Historical Society;
photograph by Jaime Reyes)

could be addressed if not represented—one page, one photo, one name, and one life at a time. This was not the heroic action of Oliver Stone's first-responders, sentimentalized and celebrated like so many valiant soldiers returning home from battle. The poignancy of the missing posters has more to do with the smallness and humility of the gestures, as well as their local character. These were expressly antiheroic images.

As a response to apocalyptic reality television, the missing-person flyers were like so many humble notes of acceptance and refusal—at once confirming and denying the spectacular betrayal of the United States by its own modern technologies. The incongruence between the flyers and the enormity of what they attempted to witness was overwhelming. As frames for the modern individual, they communicated how out of proportion the authors/witnesses were to the event—a truth that reverberated with viewers across the world. The homemade texts were more poignant to some viewers because of their superior capacity to signify death. In the words of Marianne Hirsch: "These are images of people looking toward a future they will never have. Violently yanked out of one context and inserted into a totally incongruous one, they exemplify what Roland Barthes describes as the retrospective irony of looking at photographs—the viewer possesses the deadly knowledge that the subject of the image will not know" (*Day Time Stopped* 3).

This decontextualization of family photography not only rendered the images more poignant but also left them more susceptible to political manipulation and recontextualization. As Hirsch has written elsewhere of family photographs, "Identity is no longer individual but is defined by the mask of familial relation and of photographic convention" (*Family Frames* 98). Hirsch continues, "When we are photographed in the context of the conventions of family-snapshot photography . . . we wear masks, fabricate ourselves according to certain expectations and are fabricated by them" (98). While the faces that appeared in these texts were read as personal expressions of longing and grief, Hirsch's pre-9/11 work reminds us that for so-called moderns and primitives alike, "masks are protective screens and disguises, hiding the individual faces and expressions inscribing them into a conventional narrative. But they are also ritual masks uniting the characters in the rites of family life, constituted through the camera into magic moments with mysterious, haunting and lasting power" (*Family Frames*

98). One cautious New Yorker makes a sign and leaves it next to one of the impromptu shrines in the city. The sign reads, "What will happen when the candlelight is over?"

Wanted

As early as September 17, 2001, President Bush was invoking the iconic wanted poster of the frontier imaginary as a rhetorical device for putting a face on the events of 9/11: "I want justice. There's an old poster out west, as I recall, that said, 'Wanted: Dead or Alive.' . . . I just remember, all I'm doing is remembering when I was a kid I remember that they used to put out there in the old west, a wanted poster. It said: 'Wanted, Dead or Alive.' All I want and America wants is him brought to justice. That's what we want."[9] When President Bush called for the capture of Osama bin Laden, "Dead or Alive," he placed the villain squarely within the frame of the wanted poster, but his move was somewhat redundant. Bin Laden was already a prominent member of the FBI's Ten Most Wanted list, where he had been placed in June 1999 after being indicted for murder, conspiracy, and other charges in connection with the U.S. embassy bombings in Africa. A five-million-dollar reward had been placed on his head. Bin Laden was also on a separate "Most Wanted Terrorists" list maintained by the FBI, which included twenty-five others who had been indicted in U.S. federal courts in connection with terror plots. According to *Washington Post* reporter Dan Eggen, "The listing was updated after Sept. 11, 2001, to include a higher reward of $25 million" (August 28, 2006). Strangely, the updated wanted poster makes no mention of the attacks on the Pentagon and the World Trade Center (*Washington Post,* August 29, 2006).

What sets President Bush's rhetorical allusion to a wanted poster for Osama Bin Laden apart from actual FBI posters already in circulation is his purposeful embrace of the vigilante justice of the frontier, rather than the coded sobriety of the FBI. It is also obvious from the president's choice of words that he wished to appeal to the imagined, rather than the real, wanted poster. "As I recall" places the wanted poster within the frame of popular memory, rather than American history. The president's performance of memory sloppily relocates the wanted poster to the president's childhood years: "I just remember, all I'm doing is remembering when I was a kid I remember that they used to put out there in the old west, a wanted poster. It said: 'Wanted, Dead or Alive.' " If Bush did have the childhood experience of seeing or hearing about a wanted poster out there in "the old west," it was likely a souvenir-shop wanted poster for sale in an Old West constructed and maintained by members of the tourism industry active in the Western United States at midcentury.

By performing his personal memory of reading the wanted poster as a child, the president models the mock encounter the wanted poster establishes among the reader, President Bush, and the outlaw Bin Laden. Significantly, the president positions himself as the reader, not the author, of the wanted poster. In this way he lets the American public know that he is not the law, but one of us—just a curious member of the reading public: "all I'm doing is remembering."

The president's allusion to the imagined wanted poster also accomplishes several other moves simultaneously and efficiently. It places Bush back in the Western landscape of Texas from which he hails, thereby marking him as a child of the frontier and now a full-grown cowboy. It expresses a pioneering spirit, embodied by the cowboy-in-chief, which reflects an antagonistic relationship to racial and cultural others and their landscape. It installs a Manichean worldview, based on a border violation. And it situates the listener in a story world where the only means of restoring order is violent retribution. The allusion to the Wild West organizes the world in terms of stark contrasts between good and evil, cowboys and natives, not to mention projecting a battle scene set in the desert. Perhaps most significantly, the president's allusion to the wanted poster swiftly relocates the frontier from Bin Laden's stomping grounds to the president's, from the Middle East to Texas, where he knows how things work and is in charge.[10]

By placing the wanted poster in the Wild West, Bush's rhetoric also reconnects it with historic rituals of public execution, as well as the practice of parading dead outlaws before the public. When the president says that he wants Bin Laden "brought to justice," he is saying, "Bring me Osama Bin Laden's head on a platter." Here "justice" codes for old-school vigilante justice. The extreme brutality of the terrorist attacks justifies an extremely violent response—one that must be summoned from the American past because the present-day United States is modern and therefore potentially too soft on terrorism. Notably, this also invokes the violent American ritual of the death penalty, rather than the trial. It calls for the spectacular performance of violent retribution against the body of Bin Laden. But as the American and international public would learn in the weeks, months, and years following, the bodies of other Arabic men would do as stand-ins or body doubles for Bin Laden so long as the manhunt for him proved unsuccessful.

The president's call for the capture of Bin Laden, "Dead or Alive," was consummated in the Web posting of the "secret" video of Saddam Hussein's execution by hanging. However, this was just the most prominent example of a stream of revenge tortures and killings, coupled with ritual displays of dead bodies and bodies in pain. These practices of recording and displaying violent retribution have been accompanied by a strict policy of censorship when it comes to making and sharing images that feature the bodies of maimed and dead American soldiers and contractors. Trophy photos of dead Iraqis set the parameters for the image war that also intentionally produced, but unintentionally shared, the notorious Abu Ghraib images. Other such trophy photos have featured the corpses of Saddam's sons, Al Zarqawi in a gold frame, Saddam's "medical" inspection upon capture, and the Pentagon's deck of "Iraq's Most Wanted" playing cards.[11]

This celebrated and maligned deck—a series of miniature wanted posters—has been regularly revisited in televised and printed news reports of successful captures and/or killings. The "Iraq's Most Wanted" cards represent an official use of the wanted poster as a souvenir of war. They may be interpreted as a sober cry for war, or an ironic play on the history of American war propaganda, or something in-between. The substitution of "Iraq's" for "America's" Most Wanted is disingenuous in this case. What the faces in this deck of cards show the consumer is still "America's Most Wanted." How could it be otherwise? The cards were manufactured by the military, even if ordinary citizens can purchase the deck in gas stations and quickie marts across the country. The playing cards were manufactured to be instantly collectible war propaganda. In tone the cards are closer to the lynching postcards circulated by some white Southerners during Reconstruction than they are to the official wanted posters issued by the military. But the cards are tools of war, made and circulated by the state, not by rebels. As members of "Iraq's Most Wanted" have been caught, their

"Iraq's Most Wanted" playing cards.
(Courtesy U.S. Playing Card Company)

capture and/or death has been signified by an "X" placed over the image on their card. Graphics featuring Xed-out Iraqis have appeared in numerous mainstream newspapers and online news sources.

The "Iraq's Most Wanted" playing cards are the military's version of the FBI's Most Wanted Program. The cards perform the violence of the state in a manner that is meant to appeal to the American public. The mainstream press has demonstrated its complicity with this performance by uncritically adopting the Pentagon's visual aids and ritualistically putting them on display each time a new fugitive is caught.[12] For a mainstream American audience that knows very little about Iraq, its history, culture, and people (and especially for those Americans who do not personally know any Iraqis or Iraqi Americans), the shift from America's to Iraq's Most Wanted may slip further. At worst, the deck of playing cards may criminalize all Iraqis in the eyes of those with no other points of reference.

With the phrase "I want justice," the president also mouthed the desire of the American people for justice and suggested the death penalty as the answer. At the same time, by invoking the Wild West, the president went in drag as the cowboy vigilante, thereby passing the violence of the state off as the violence of the rugged individual of the frontier. Cowboy drag plays particularly well to a subset of the president's base: the law-and-order, libertarian, and militiaman wing of the Republican Party.[13] The cowboy "uniform" is a brilliant disguise because it signifies a palatable brand of authoritarianism for many Americans. The cowboy is a secular image of righteous violence. By rhetorically donning the cowboy's uniform, the president is able to put on innocence even as he straps on his six-shooter. The cowboy's popular appeal issues from his legendary association with natives. The cowboy is expressly not the lawman or the soldier. This is not the fascist aesthetics that Susan Sontag worries over as a form of camp-gone-awry. In contrast to the dark eroticism of the SS uniform, the authoritarian American hero puts on a white hat and chaps. He is not pictured inside an undisclosed prison or interrogation chamber, but outside in the open air of a bright sunny landscape, backed by a blue sky, sitting proudly on his horse, wearing a wry smile.

Within the visual economy established by the iconic wanted poster of the frontier imaginary, the terrorist, who is purportedly primitive in his beliefs, practices, and methods of fighting, draws the primitive out of the cowboy president. Bin Laden, and later Saddam Hussein, are at once Bush's alibi and his target. The coding of "the terrorists" as primitive sets the stage for the United States' uptake of the rough tactics and visceral violence of the Old West. One need look no further than the Internet traffic in both still and moving images of extreme violence—beheadings, torture, murder, and execution—for ample proof.

Some Americans were quick to embrace the coded racism of the president's rhetoric of righteous violence and began fashioning their own wanted posters. Some were posted on personal Web pages; others were stamped on city streets and walls, hung in places of business or leisure, and displayed in private homes. The racism and xenophobia implicit in the president's "cowboy rhetoric" become explicit and visible in the vernacular wanted posters made and circulated in response to the president's words.[14] In these images it is Bin Laden's alien status as an ethnic and religious other that is on display. It is almost as if he appears costumed as an Arab, and ironically, his costume recalls Christian biblical imagery. Vernacular renditions of Bin

"The Faces of Global Terrorism." (Courtesy U.S. State Department, http://www.state.gov/documents/organization/77420.pdf)

Laden reveal the wanted poster as an ethnocentric apparatus of perception. "It isn't simply that every Arab face is reduced to a mug shot," writes Amitava Kumar. "It's also that any other mug shot will *also* be assumed to be that of an Arab" (3). This is because the mug shot "turns aliens . . . into lawbreakers, if not also terrorists" (Kumar 40).

Bin Laden became the face of terror but also—and perhaps more compellingly to the Bush Administration—the face of antiglobalization, which aligned him with those troublesome natives who were perceived as an obstacle to the expansion of the American frontier in the nineteenth century. If the domestic outlaws featured on wanted posters in the United States have ritualistically reinforced possessive individualism by signifying its inverse, then the faces of terror have ritualistically reinforced American imperialism in the postcolonial era. The most wanted terrorists could also accurately be labeled the most wanted members of the antiglobalization movement.

American Innocence

According to the anthropologist Victor Turner, "Every social drama entails a loss of innocence, compensated for by a gain in experiential knowledge" ("Image" 248). But gains in experiential knowledge are not consistent with or even desirable to those who would preserve cherished American myths. In her analysis of the popular appeal of the term "Ground Zero" in discourses surrounding 9/11, Marita Sturken argues, "Throughout most of the nation's history, U.S. self-image has remained firmly wedded to a kind of isolationist innocence, so that virtually every traumatic event of 20th-century U.S. history, from Pearl Harbor to the Vietnam War, has been characterized as the moment when that innocence was lost" ("Aesthetics" 311). Wherever the cultural narrative of innocence lost is invoked to explain the events of 9/11, this claim is always made, either explicitly or implicitly, in relation to the fact that the attacks occurred on American soil. Somehow American claims to innocence lost depend on the perception that a geographic and symbolic boundary was crossed in the attacks. This is a crucial point because it is this articulation—between a perceived boundary violation and innocence lost—that made 9/11 ripe for cooptation by the gendered and racist ideologies and iconography of the frontier imaginary.

Swept up in the cultural narrative of innocence lost and the iconography of vigilante justice, the missing-person flyers and other victim displays became signs of national innocence. These texts were prized precisely because their claim on innocence was not overtly nationalist. Initially, they made claims only for the innocence of particular victims of terrorism and from within familial and personal networks, rather than nationalist rhetoric and ideology. They made perfect political instruments insofar as they attested to America's innocence and did so in a manner that was—at least at the time of their making—perfectly innocent of political motivation. For readers not familiar with the particular individuals pictured, the flyers invoked the figure of the missing child, who starred as the primary figure of innocence and functioned as a recurrent prompt to moral anxiety within the American imaginary during the 1980s and 1990s.

In time the loss of particular individuals was generalized and culturally coded as the lost childhood of the nation. Curated displays of the missing-person flyers (not to mention repeated invocations of the victims by cultural authorities) addressed readers and listeners as insiders, members of a moral community of suffering and shared trauma. This address cannot be understood as standing outside of or apart from the conservative embrace of the white child victim in the 1980s and 1990s, in whose name calls were made for greater police power and harsher sentencing. In effect, Americans had been conditioned by the law-and-order discourse and victim displays of the 1980s and 1990s to respond to portraits of the missing with "uncritical outrage" (Sturken, "Image" 192).

American vernacular, governmental, and media practices of "facing" the events of 9/11 installed a new field of social relations between people and images in which the missing and the wanted functioned as "go-betweens" and "scapegoats" for American readers who were fast becoming vigilante viewers for the "war on terror" (W. J. T. Mitchell 46). Westerners often assume that "putting a face" on an issue or problem humanizes it, but according to Gilles Deleuze and Felix Guattari, facialization is an ethnocentric visual technology allowing the perpetual renewal of Western claims to and eroticization of innocence through Judeo-Christian identifications with violent physical suffering:

> The face is not a universal. It is not even that of the white
> man; it is White Man himself, with his broad white cheeks
> and the black hole of his eyes. The face is Christ. The face
> is the typical European, what Ezra Pound classed the aver-

age sensual man, in short, the ordinary, everyday Eroto-
maniac (nineteenth-century psychiatrists were right to say
that erotomania, unlike nymphomania, often remains pure
and chaste; this is because it operates through the face and
facialization). . . Jesus Christ superstar: he invented the facialization of the entire body and spread it everywhere (the
Passion of Joan of Arc, in close-up). (176)

Writing about the American response to 9/11, Judith Butler also challenged
the assumption that the effect of putting a face on a historical event or social
problem is always a benign process: "We may think of the different ways
that violence can happen: one is precisely *through* the production of the
face, the face of Osama bin Laden, the face of Yasser Arafat, the face of
Saddam Hussein" (141).

The characters starring in the "war on terror" were not the gangster and
the G-man of the original "war on crime," but "the victims of 9/11" and
"the terrorists." The Bush Administration's repeated references to the
villains and victims of 9/11 served a performance of what political scientist
Jamie Mayerfeld calls "extreme realism"—the belief that unless we respond
to the terrorists in a maximal fashion, we must not care about the innocents
lost.[15] The "unless" here points to the rightness and righteousness of the
extreme measures that would be, must be, taken. To those defending civil
liberties, extreme realism says: "Get real. We live in a different world now.
Everything has changed."

In the space between these conventional ways of framing the modern
and purportedly premodern individual, the reader gains access to the symbolic boundaries between life and death, personhood and property, "civilized" and "primitive," or what Georgio Agamben calls the "state of exception" and terrorism. Images of the missing and the wanted serve as
compelling yet comfortingly familiar evidence for claims that Americans are
living in a terrifying new world. The wanted posters addressed readers
as citizen-surveyors and solicited surveillance of "foreigners" and fellow
Americans (the enemy within) as a form of good citizenship. The missing
notices were not entirely disconnected from practices of domestic and
neighborhood surveillance. Marita Sturken argues that photographs of
missing children "ask us to engage with them not as personal images,

snapshots of the past, but rather as participants in an investigation. Citizenship is defined through these images as the active surveillance of one's neighbors, always on the lookout for suspicious groupings of individuals and potential missing children under cover" ("Image" 191–92).

The representation of 9/11 through the framing devices of the wanted poster and the missing notice helped an authoritarian leader and his administration obscure their questionable and in some cases illegal or extralegal practices in prosecuting the "war on terror." By "facing" 9/11, the Bush Administration shifted the burden of proof from itself to the American public. The wanted poster and the missing notice caught the reading public in a bind: either they submitted to the masculine authority of the federal government and the military and played the role of the victims who survived, which entailed suspending their right to question that authority if they wanted protection from future attacks, or they refused to submit and thereby risked being framed as terrorists.

It is not that Americans were duped by the president's "cowboy rhetoric." Rather, the cultural frames deployed subtly recast the field of social relations in the everyday lives of Americans. Images of the "missing" and the "wanted" infantilized Americans and made suspects of them at the same time. Americans were caught in a perpetual oscillation of identification between the perpetrators and the victims of terrorism: "If you're not with us, you're against us." Contributing to the war effort required Americans to submit to new, expanded forms of surveillance at home, while the U.S. military safeguarded the economic interests of American elites abroad —a deadly pursuit that had little if anything to do with the material threats faced by ordinary Americans.

NOTES

Introduction

1. Police texts belong to what film theorist Bill Nichols calls "the discourses of sobriety" (3). Science, economics, politics, foreign policy, education, religion—these are some examples of disciplines that speak from within the discourses of sobriety. They are united by an instrumental orientation to the real and are seldom, if ever, receptive to "make-believe" characters, events, or entire worlds. The discourses of sobriety are sobering, Nichols tells us, because they regard their relation to the real as "direct, immediate, transparent. Through them power exerts itself. Through them, things are made to happen" (4).

2. The wanted poster for Grover Cleveland Bergdoll is not only the first known "wanted" poster, but the oldest poster in the FBI's collection.

3. The matter of tracking the wanted poster's formal development is tricky because many different individuals and organizations made and circulated them. Over the latter half of the nineteenth century and into the early part of the twentieth, parties issuing reward notices included express companies, post offices, local police, national police, international police, banks, mayor's offices, wardens, railroad companies and lines, district attorneys, and other private companies like jewelers. Suffice it to say there was no standardization across these texts. I treat the practices of Pinkerton's National Detective Agency as representative for two reasons: first, their posters circulated nationally and so would likely have influenced local practices in regions across the country; second, the agency was a clearinghouse for notices made elsewhere and so would have kept pace with local innovations in the text's formal development.

4. Approved on May 18, 1917, the Selective Service Law "required all able bodied men ages 21 to 30 (later extended to ages 18 to 45) to register for the draft regardless of race or religion" (http://www.army.mil/-news/2007/06/03/3099-registration-day-a-spiritual-awakening/).

5. Military recruitment posters were the earliest American broadsides to feature the word "WANTED" as a heading. See, e.g., a Civil War–era recruitment poster issued in Boston on July 22, 1864. In bold type and all caps, the top third of the broadside reads: "500,000 MEN / WANTED." The broadside belongs to the

Printed Ephemera Collection at the Library of Congress (http://hdl.loc.gov/loc.rbc/rbpe.07101500).

6. See "The Most Famous Poster," in American Treasures of the Library of Congress (http://www.loc.gov/exhibits/treasures/trm015.html).

7. Following the lead of Bruno Latour and Catherine Porter, who argue that perhaps we were never modern, William J. T. Mitchell asserts that moderns and postmoderns in the "developed" world regularly indulge in and are at times plagued by magical thinking when it comes to images. Given this, he wants two things from visual studies scholars: to admit that they treat images like quasi-animate beings and to allow this recognition to open onto analyses of mutually constitutive networks made up of people and images. Unlike in Debord's formulation of a social network of people, mediated by images, Mitchell grants people and images equal status. Mitchell offers this new method of visual critique, which he calls totemism, as an alternative to iconoclastic criticism. Mitchell characterizes this reorientation of criticism as a matter of sounding idols rather than smashing icons.

8. In media studies the word *spectator* is reserved for the film audience and carries, in particular, the theoretical heft and critical missteps of psychoanalytic film theory. The term *viewer* is typically reserved for the television audience and connotes the home viewer's divided attention by comparison to the rapt attention of the film viewer, cloaked in the darkness of the theater and committed to watching the film straight through from beginning to end. I use the term *spectator* and refer to the vigilante viewer as a mode of spectatorship because of the distance it connotes between those watching and those doing. My use of this term indicates the status of outlaw displays as minor spectacles and is not intended to activate the theoretical paradigms of psychoanalytic film theory. I use the term *viewer* to describe a divided, mobile practice of looking that also often involves reading. In practice the vigilante viewer confronts outlaw displays in passing. She is a mobile spectator, and the ephemeral status of the circular does not ask of her what a film might. Finally, I use the term *viewer* because its association with television indicates an interactive practice between the viewer and the medium, in which the viewer has more discretion over where her attention is directed and how long it lights on a particular outlaw display.

9. Cynthia Enloe describes this as the "womenandchildren-protected-by-statesmen" scenario (96). Dana Cloud talks about this as "the white man's burden" within imperialist discourse: "The white man's burden is a core element in narratives of clashes between white, Western societies and inferior Others requiring policing and rescue" (286).

10. C. B. MacPherson's political theory of possessive individualism explains how the economic status of property ownership has shaped the concept of individualism in the liberal tradition. In the political theories of liberal thinkers, MacPherson argues, ownership is constitutive of individuality, freedom, and equality. Society is

made up of relations among independent owners, and the primary role of government is to "protect owners against illegitimate incursions upon their property and to maintain conditions of orderly exchange" (Carens 2).

11. Foucault writes in *Discipline and Punish:* "But the punishment-body relation is not the same as it was in the torture during public executions. The body now serves as an instrument or intermediary: if one intervenes upon it to imprison it, or to make it work, it is in order to deprive the individual of a liberty that is regarded both as a right and as a property" (11).

12. The racialized visual culture of the frontier imaginary continues to shape the production, circulation, and reception of missing notices today. This is true despite the fact that "many of the children whose images are circulated as missing children have either run away from home or have been 'abducted' by one of their parents in a custody battle" (Sturken, "Image" 190).

13. The outlaw has served as a romantic figure of liminality in academic as well as popular cultures. Michael Bowman notes that scholars of performance and cultural studies have embraced the outlaw/trickster as a figure of liminality. Citing Donna Harraway's work, he calls scholars to account for their theoretical romance with the outlaw: "But I wonder sometimes whether we in performance and cultural studies are interested in talking to a *real* Coyote" (363).

14. Foucault uses Jeremy Bentham's prison design for the Panopticon as a model of modern disciplinary power reduced to its ideal form. The Panopticon, he argues, is an active architecture, capable of realizing surveillance and resultant self-discipline (*Discipline* 202). Specifically, Bentham's structure arranges prisoners in a ring around a central prison tower, encouraging each man to discipline himself because at any given moment the guard *might* be watching him. If public spectacles of torture promoted social order by showing members of the crowd the excruciating pain and suffering that would befall them should they defy the powers that be, then modern mechanisms of surveillance encourage individuals to imagine that they might be being observed by the authorities and, therefore, to self-regulate.

15. In 1964 Warhol was one of ten artists invited to decorate the facade of the New York State Pavilion at the World's Fair in Flushing Meadow. He created a mural entitled *Thirteen Most Wanted Men.* Warhol reproduced frontal and profile mug shots of wanted criminals on an epic scale appropriate to the World's Fair. Each panel measured four feet by four feet (Meyer, *Outlaw Representation* 128–45). Arranged into a grid, the profile shots alternated with frontal shots, creating a new relay of gazes between the men thus displayed. Art historian Richard Meyer reads the visual pattern of *Thirteen Most Wanted Men* as Warhol's technique for creating a visual link between homoeroticism and criminality (*Outlaw Representation* 137). It should also be noted that Warhol's choice to turn the wanted men to face each other introduces the possibility of the vigilante viewer's exclusion, underscoring her desire not to be cut off from the flow of serial images of crime and punishment—a

threat realized forty-eight hours later, when the mural was painted over with silver aluminum house paint. For an in-depth discussion of the work's censorship, see Richard Meyer's book *Outlaw Representation.*

16. Tony Bennett critiques Foucault's pronouncement of the end of displays of power as an "incautious generalization." He writes: "For it by no means follows from the fact that punishment had ceased to be a spectacle that the function of displaying power—of making it visible for all to see—had itself fallen into abeyance" (65). In *The Birth of the Museum: History, Theory, Politics,* Bennett argues that the exhibitionary complex developed over roughly the same period of time as that of the Panopticon; however, the technology of vision it installed worked in the reverse direction. As punishment was moving behind closed doors, the exhibitionary complex was involved in the transfer of objects previously closed up in private and semiprivate domains into more public arenas (60–61). Along similar lines Donovan argues that the relationship between spectacle and surveillance is no longer best understood in terms of competing modes of visual culture. Rather, she argues, spectacle and surveillance ought to be understood in terms of their "mutual dependence" (119).

ONE. *Execution Broadsides*

1. "In terms of sheer size," writes Dwight Conquergood, "executions were the most popular performance genre in seventeenth- and eighteenth-century America" (344).

2. Cohen notes that this practice reveals awareness, on the part of religious leaders, that the public's attraction to gallows literature exceeded its capacity to exemplify religious doctrine (7–10).

3. Woodcuts, the earliest form of printed illustration, were first used in the mid-fifteenth century (http://www.nls.uk/broadsides/broadside.cfm/id/14482).

4. According to the National Library of Scotland, the fiddle is on display in the Clan MacPherson museum in Newtonmore, Inverness-shire.

5. During the early eighteenth century printers introduced new crime genres. Cohen labels these conversion narratives, execution accounts, trial reports, newspaper stories, and crime ballads (13). He argues that these developments reflected more general trends in New England society. As British authorities began to exert more control over the colonies, New England printers turned more and more to English literary models (13).

6. Execution broadsides vanished at the beginning of the nineteenth century. Cohen attributes this to the rise of the penny press in the 1830s and the gradual abolition of public executions on a state-by-state basis over the course of the nineteenth and early twentieth centuries (25).

7. Elizabeth Clark argues that as the popular appeal of the passion of Christ waned, and anesthesia made pain avoidable for the first time in the history of the

body, physical suffering no longer held the moral value it once had. Americans began to interpret pain not as integral to human experience, but as "flowing from the breach of a natural law" (473). Hence, pain was shifted "from the realm of normal experience and toward the status of an anomaly" (473).

TWO. *Slave Notices*

1. In some parts of Europe debtors were also pictured as a means of public shaming. Samuel Edgerton (1985) traces this practice to the thirteenth century in Northern Italy. The Italian "defaming picture," or *pittura infamante*, was "an officially sanctioned insulting portrait of a guilty citizen in contempt of court and out of reach of the local constabulary" (15). The guilty person's effigy was painted in a public setting so that all members of the community could witness his humiliation and potentially pressure him to turn himself in and repent. Edgerton demonstrates that many famous Florentine artists participated in this popular defaming art, which flourished in Florence between the thirteen and sixteenth centuries (15).

2. Interestingly, the earliest recorded case of one man posting another for an offense against property appeared in the *Guardian* in 1633 and involved a contest waged over the body of a woman: "If you take the wench now, I'll have it posted first, then chronicled, Thou wert beaten to it" (*Oxford English Dictionary* 182). Encapsulated in this threat are both a demand for justice (the possibility of recourse to an impartial witness) and the desperate expression of thwarted desire: its author intends to publicly lament his failed acquisition.

3. "$500 Reward," 1835, Portfolio 24, Folder 13, *Broadsides, leaflets, and pamphlets from America and Europe,* Printed Ephemera Collection, Library of Congress, Washington, D.C.

4. In the eighteenth century alone planters wishing to retrieve some 2,002 slaves placed 1,863 runaway notices in the *South Carolina Gazette* and other colonial newspapers. See Meaders.

5. See E. Clark.

6. See J. D. Hall.

7. Manigault Family Papers, Series 1, Plantation Records 1833–1877, Folder 5, Southern Historical Collection, Manuscripts Department, Library of the University of North Carolina, Chapel Hill.

8. When the hunt for Dolly proved unsuccessful, Manigault pasted the runaway notice into the back of a plantation ledger for safekeeping. A professional collector named J. G. Roulhac Hamilton later acquired the notice for the Southern Historical Collection at the University of North Carolina. See *Southern Sources.*

9. While Manigault kept the runaway notice as a highly personal response to the Civil War and the changes it wrought, the library reads his practices of record keeping and collection as exemplary of slaveholders' behavior on plantations throughout the South. The exhibition catalog, *Southern Sources,* reports that the

Manigault Family Papers "illustrate the nature of slavery on plantations located throughout the South" (95).

10. See Meaders. A whole subgenre of runaway notices treats the fugitive more like a missing child than like a runaway slave (Meaders 296).

11. See Willis and Williams for a discussion of the gendered and raced politics of stripping the men and women photographed by Zealy.

12. According to Trachtenberg, the emulatory photos of "illustrious Americans" made by Brady during this era were self-consciously generalized so as to avoid the charge of mere likeness. Brady was intent on elevating photographic portraiture to the level of art and defending his work against the charge that photography was merely mechanical. Portraiture was not in vogue at the time. Historical and allegorical subjects held sway. Sentimental in its attempt to bring and hold the nation together, the collection included representatives of all political persuasions, unified by the shared designation of "illustrious Americans."

13. M. N. Mitchell argues that the portraits of redeemed slave girls were so appealing because they put a white face on Emancipation. The images reassured white viewers that "the postbellum United States, despite its millions of black inhabitants, would remain a white nation" (399).

14. See McCauley 27–30. McCauley argues that the card grew out of two contradictory impulses: to rival painted portraiture and lend an air of serious art to photography and to capitalize on photography's ability to capture likeness rapidly and cheaply for the purposes of identification and documentation.

15. Email correspondence, Apr. 23, 2005.

16. For a more extended discussion of the historical relationship between Dolly and Louis Manigault, particularly as it pertains to his treatment of her as family property, see my essay "Missing Dolly."

17. See Wiegman.

18. According to Walter Benjamin, the nineteenth century viewed order as the absence of disease and death. Westerners wanted to clean up social space by removing death from sight (*Illuminations* 93–94). Historian Elizabeth Clark argues that it was not only corpses but also bodies in pain that became newly objectionable in the nineteenth century. Clark attributes decreased tolerance for spectacles of pain to significant developments in religious and medical thought (473).

19. Kirk Fuoss estimates that between 1882 and 1939, a total of 5,125 lynchings occurred in the United States (2).

20. Peter Ehrenhaus and Susan Owen argue that Christians did not uniformly abandon the passion of Christ. Those who held onto the crucifixion as the centerpiece of Christian faith did so through the spectacular torture and murder of African Americans. In effect, lynching was a ritual reenactment of the passion of Christ, which ironically substituted a black body for one imagined as white. Whereas social reformers defined order as the absence of death and disease, white supremacists defined order as the continued power to brutalize and expunge those who did not belong.

21. According to Wiegman, "Both mainstream and alternative newspapers regularly ran stories documenting the scenes of violence, often offering graphic detail of the practices of torture through which the entire African-American population could be defined and policed as innately, if no longer legally inferior" (91).

THREE. *Pinkerton Posters*

1. During these years urban populations in America grew by 79 percent. As people emigrated from Europe, cities became less and less homogenous. In the 1830s, 1840s, and 1850s, urban uprisings proved the inability of the old system to deal with such problems and prompted the modern police movement to make its way across the country. In 1844 New York was the first city to respond by forming a modern police force modeled on the London Metropolitan Police. Over the next thirteen years Cincinnati, New Orleans, Boston, Philadelphia, Chicago, and Baltimore soon followed suit. By 1860 most major cities in the United States had a modern police force (Morn 26). Even after the onset of the modern police movement in the United States, rural, national, and international crime fighting remained the job of private citizens and agencies.

2. Their practices of looking reflected the visual culture of the exhibitionary complex: "While everyone could see, there were also vantage points from which everyone could be seen" (Bennett 65). As defined by Tony Bennett, the exhibitionary complex refers to the nineteenth-century emergence of art, history, and natural science museums; dioramas and panoramas; national and, later, international exhibitions; and arcades and department stores.

3. Jennifer Green-Lewis describes this perhaps unintended consequence of professional outlaw displays in reference to Byrnes's volume: "Notwithstanding their attention to individual narratives, the organizational method within which subject photographs of criminal or psychic aberrancy are contextualized and thus made reader ready predetermines the purpose of reading as classificatory. Just as readers are to affirm their own unlikeness from the pictures and thus to register themselves, in the most elementary way, as distinct from those persons imaged, so they are enabled to perceive likenesses between pictures and thus implicitly to consent to the existence of a group whose theoretical existence photography proves to be grounded in material signs" (216).

4. The body of law related to embezzlement was yet to be created; hence, accusations of theft and larceny required proof of trespass (Morn 18).

5. The famous all-seeing-eye design first appeared on a set of lamps Pinkerton commissioned for the new offices (Morn 65). Soon thereafter it would be emblazoned on the company's letterhead. Pinkerton's claimed that the popular expression "private eye" originated with the company's insignia.

6. Several editions of *General Principles* are housed with the Pinkerton collection in the Manuscripts Division of the Library of Congress (Box 54, Pinkerton's National Detective Agency Records). My discussion concerns the first edition, pub-

lished in 1878. The book was required reading for every person who worked for the agency until 1953, when it was discontinued. A second edition was published on Jan. 1, 1916, cosigned by Allan Pinkerton and his son William A. Pinkerton. There is a handwritten note in the second edition indicating that it was discontinued on June 30, 1953.

7. In the rules governing detective work, he outlines regulations for what kind of information detectives should collect, how they should go about obtaining it, and in what manner and to whom they were to report. He informs Pinkerton operatives that "under no circumstances" were they permitted to snoop through the agency's case files—not even for those cases on which they were working. Operatives were also forbidden direct contact with the agency's clients. There was a strict hierarchy of command controlling the flow and direction of information sharing, as well as a bureaucratic obsession with documentation. In order to guard against distortion and forgetting, Pinkerton operatives were required to prepare written reports after giving oral reports to their superiors. Allan Pinkerton instructed operatives to write their reports as though their superiors had not been in attendance at the first telling.

8. Likewise, Allan Sekula describes this phenomenon as "a Galilean vision of the world as a book 'written in the language of mathematics' " (17).

9. The experience of massive railroad strikes in the summer of 1877 had proven that America's public police were not equipped to maintain crowd control under such circumstances. The states involved in railroad strikes during the summer of 1877 included West Virginia, Maryland, Pennsylvania, Illinois, and Missouri (Morn 96).

10. The National Guard movement was initiated to answer to the problem of chaos caused by labor activism. Between 1877 and 1892 the National Guard was called to help in thirty-three labor disturbances and fourteen riots (Morn 97).

11. Box 55, Pinkerton's National Detective Agency Records.

12. This story is paraphrased from the official version published by Pinkerton's, ca. 1920, as part of its promotional materials. The agency had large, bookmark-style, color reproductions of the painting made up, with the story printed on the back.

13. In the 1920 version *Hands Up* was first hung in the Owl Café in 1888, but on Pinkerton's Web site the agency claims that William A. Pinkerton first set eyes on the watercolor in 1880. In the Web version of the story, the unknown "cowboy artist" gets a name, Ludke, and a nationality, German. According to the Pinkerton's Web site, he was well known in the Western states as the "Great Boy Artist," not the "cowboy artist," as he is called in the earlier version. Finally, in the Web version of the story, the Owl Café in Spokane morphs into a saloon and "noted sporting resort."

14. This information appears in "Pinkerton History" on the Pinkerton Burns International Security Services Web site (accessed Feb. 12, 2003).

15. It is unclear whether this happened before or after Allan Pinkerton's death in 1884.

16. Box 55, Pinkerton's National Detective Agency Records.

17. Although Pinkerton never subscribed to the notion of a biologically distinct criminal class, or the idea that a criminal could be recognized based on his looks, he did slip into using the term "criminal class" from time to time. And it is evident from the employee surveillance and strike-breaking work his agency performed that Pinkerton believed the working classes to be particularly prone, or at least tempted, to illegal appropriation and destruction of industrial and commercial property.

18. While the conventions of the anthropological mug shot were already in use in the 1850s, the tightly cropped front and side shots did not become standard police practice until the 1880s. By that time the head-on view had become the accepted format of populist and amateur snapshots, but also of photographic documents like prison records and social surveys (Sekula 37).

19. Box 89, Pinkerton's National Detective Agency Records.

20. The Bertillon system involved the use of steel calipers and compasses to measure heads, ears, hands, fingers, and other physical features of those arrested for criminal behavior. Bertillon calculated the odds of two people having the same measurements as one in four million. In the first three years of the system's use in the French police system, eight hundred suspects were identified. Bertillonage was enthusiastically received in the United States, and it wasn't long before police forces around the world were using the system. The Bertillon system of criminal identification was commonly used in the United States until the late 1910s and early 1920s, when it was supplanted by a superior system of identification developed at Scotland Yard: fingerprinting (Buckland and Evans 20; Sekula 25–37).

21. Unlike the photogravures and Woodburytypes that preceded them, half-tone plates enabled the economical and limitless reproduction of photographs in books, magazines, advertisements, newspapers, and posters. According to John Tagg, the half-tone plate recast the entire economy of image production: "the era of throw away images had begun" (56–57).

22. This was not an isolated incident. Jennifer Green-Lewis writes that newsman George Grantham Bain's collection of criminal photos rivaled Thomas Byrnes's collection. During the late nineteenth and early twentieth centuries, Bain's news agency routinely gathered photos of police activities and mug shots (Green-Lewis 210).

23. Box 168, Pinkerton's National Detective Agency Records.

24. Richard E. Meyer argues that in the South of the Reconstruction era, banks and trains were "symbols of the forces which kept the common man in economic and social bondage." Later, in the Midwest during the Great Depression, absentee ownership over banks and railroads elicited comparable scorn from locals ("Outlaw" 97). Likewise, Richard White notes that social bandits tended to avoid robbing the poor and individuals of any kind and concentrated their efforts on railroads and banks instead. "Thus," he writes, "they not only avoided directly harming local people, but they also preyed upon institutions that many farmers believed were preying on them" (393).

25. Eric Hobsbawm, the foremost expert on banditry, writes that social bandits "resist the encroaching power of outside authority and capital" (9).

FOUR. *The FBI's Most Wanted*

1. The widespread attention and excitement garnered by the case marked the beginnings of a dramatic rise in the popular appeal of tabloids during the 1920s. In 1919 two new publications appeared on newsstands within weeks of one another that would profoundly influence journalism, advertising, and popular culture more generally. *True Story Magazine* and the *Daily News* were picture-laden publications aimed primarily at young, working-class women. Their mass appeal quickly extended beyond this initial audience. The immense popularity of these publications —as well as their imitators, the *Daily Mirror,* the *Daily Graphic,* and other new city-based picture papers—attested to a readership that advertisers quickly labeled the "tabloid audience" (Marchand 53–59).

2. See *New York Times,* Jan. 8, 1920.

3. In newspaper coverage of the case, Grover's mother emerges as the "real" outlaw who battles the federal police over the body of her son. According to the *New York Times,* Mrs. Bergdoll met the authorities head-on, fiercely guarding the first floor of her home, while her son lay hidden in a window-box seat situated in a remote corner of the mansion's second floor: "Mrs. Bergdoll threatened death to any officer who entered her home when they appeared at the mansion today, Federal agents said." The article goes on to detail Mrs. Bergdoll's stash of weaponry: "A search of the house in which she lived showed it to be a veritable arsenal. In addition to a three-foot stack of pro-German pamphlets, the Federal agents found in the dining room a 12-guage automatic pump gun, with a large supply of shells handy. On the oak buffet were seven boxes of shells for the 38-calibre revolver with which she threatened the invaders. There was also an automatic rifle with a silencer attachment, a large dagger and other weapons. All were confiscated" (*New York Times,* Jan. 8, 1920).

4. Robert McClaughry, the warden of the Illinois State Penitentiary, first implemented policing on behalf of an imagined American public at the World's Columbian Exposition in 1893. He anticipated that the exposition's large-scale spectacle and consumer-oriented showcase would create a new form of vulnerability to criminal activity: a veritable mass of distracted viewers and shoppers ready for the taking. (Walter Benjamin calls these distracted viewers "rubbernecks" in *The Arcades Project.*) In order to guard against the anticipated crime fest, McClaughry recruited two hundred or more detectives from across the United States to serve as members of a secret service to work the exposition. As a result of McCaughry's efforts at the Columbian Exposition, the National Organization of the Chiefs of Police (soon to become the International Association of Chiefs of Police [IACP]) was formed that same year (Morn 123).

5. See Ruth; Marchand.

6. The fingerprint system first entered the United States by way of the 1904 St. Louis Exposition, where John Ferrier and James Parke of Scotland Yard put the new

technology on display (Cole 149). Scotland Yard had learned fingerprinting from Sir William Herschel, who brought the practice home from his colonial outpost in India. The chief administrative officer in Bengal, Herschel had begun experimenting with the use of fingerprints for identification purposes around the same time that Alphonse Bertillon developed his anthropometric system (Cohn 11). Herschel, who was said to have learned fingerprinting from the Bengalis, later used the technique against them. Once Herschel and his fellow administrators discovered that Bengalis were collecting government pensions by impersonating deceased pensioners, they wanted to put a stop to the practice, but they could not distinguish rightful claimants from impersonators based on looks alone (Cole 64). In other words, the success of Bengalis who claimed pensions on behalf of the dead relied upon the racist vision of colonial officers who were unable to tell them apart.

7. Fingerprinting made it possible to decipher and then rank individual criminals, but it also made it practical to collect information on individual members of criminalized or otherwise degraded populations. In 1910 the Inferior Criminal Courts Act ordered magistrates' courts in New York City to fingerprint all prostitutes who entered the system, making them the first criminal population to be fingerprinted in the United States. The method was embraced over Bertillonage because it involved less physical contact between police clerks and prostitutes. At the time the physical closeness and contact required to take a prisoner's Bertillon measurements were considered inappropriate for arrested women (Cole 154–55).

8. The U.S. Army is a case in point. Beginning in 1906, recruits were fingerprinted upon entering the service. Fingerprints were used to identify deserters, repeat enlisters, or men dishonorably discharged who sought to reenlist (Cole 153–62).

9. This situation was not merely the product of Hoover's rhetoric; it was also due to a new reality: automobiles had made it possible for professional thieves to quickly cross state lines in order to escape local police. The automobile, not Hoover, had nationalized criminal activity, he argued. The FBI was merely responding to the new social problems created by the automobile.

10. See Potter on how the FBI sold this idea to the public.

11. In *State of Exception* Georgio Agamben writes: "Because the sovereign power of the President is essentially grounded in the emergency linked to a state of war, over the course of the twentieth century the metaphor of war becomes an integral part of the presidential vocabulary whenever decisions considered to be of vital importance are being imposed" (21).

12. According to Ruth, "Hoover's FBI helped concentrate the nation's attention on bandits like Dillinger and Pretty Boy Floyd, who targeted poorly protected small-town banks." The author suggests that the gangster's movement to the country was a Depression-era phenomenon (145–46).

13. See Potter for a detailed account of the creation of G-men and gangsters as popular heroes of the era.

14. The moralistic textual frame imposed on the popular film *The Public Enemy* is exemplary of this dynamic. The foreword to the film reads: "It is the ambition of the authors of *'The Public Enemy'* to honestly depict an environment that exists today in a certain strata of American life, rather than glorify the hoodlum or the criminal. While the story of *'The Public Enemy'* is essentially a true story, all names and characters appearing herein, are purely fictional.—*Warner Bros. Pictures, Inc.*" After the film's powerful and shocking conclusion, another text rolls: "The end of Tom Powers is the end of every hoodlum. 'The Public Enemy' is not a man, nor is it a character—it is a problem that sooner or later WE, the public, must solve." The foreword to the 1954 re-release collapses the frame: "Perhaps the toughest of the gangster films, 'Public Enemy' and 'Little Caesar' had a great effect on public opinion. They brought home violently the evils associated with prohibition and suggested the necessity of a nation-wide house cleaning. Tom Powers in 'Public Enemy' and Rico in 'Little Caesar' are not two men, nor are they merely characters— they are a problem that sooner or later we, the public, must solve."

15. These are conclusions reached in conversations with the FBI's acting historian, John Fox, in Jan. 2004.

16. When matching prints were discovered, the new set was sent to an "assembly section where the complete record of the individual was assembled, rechecked, and consolidated" (Hoover 210). The final step was for the typing clerks to prepare letters and telegrams informing all interested officials of the discovery and contents of the newly consolidated record.

17. David Ruth notes the sharp contrast between pop-cultural depictions of law enforcement in the 1920s and early 1930s and stories and images circulated about Hoover's FBI: "In the twenties and early thirties criminals highlighted official weakness, ineptitude, and corruption. Powerful, technologically sophisticated mobsters blithely ignored stereotyped backward Irish flatfoots, underpowered patrol cars, and a toothless federal government. This relationship changed dramatically after the media coronation of J. Edgar Hoover and his G-Men as the nation's crime busters. A series of highly publicized outlaws, John Dillinger the most important, served as foils to the newly potent federal crime fighters. Cast as supporting characters in modern morality plays, these criminals contributed to a timely, hopeful message about a new federal effectiveness in responding to urgent national problems" (145).

18. In some cases, if the mug shots or other available photographs had been taken years ago, this was noted next to the images. The purpose was to encourage those looking for the wanted person to imagine an aged version of the one pictured.

19. Collections of these publications can be found at the FBI archives in Washington, D.C.

20. Hoover outlines the intended functions of the new bulletin as follows: "It is intended that this publication should provide a clearing house for police officials regarding successful police methods, a medium for the dissemination of important

police information, and a comprehensive literature pertaining to the scientific methods in crime detection and crime apprehension" (*FBI Law Enforcement Bulletin* 4, no. 10 [Oct. 1, 1935], FBI Archives).

21. Tabloid coverage of crime and punishment entered a new phase of morbid realism in 1928. On Friday, Jan. 13, the *New York Daily News*, "New York's Picture Newspaper," published a photograph of Ruth Snyder being electrocuted. The front-page headline read, "DEAD!" The paper boasted that it was the first to let America see a woman die in the electric chair. A wife and mother, Snyder had been condemned with her lover for strangling and bludgeoning her husband to death. Twenty-four people witnessed her execution that day. Twenty of the witnesses were newspapermen, but photographers were specifically barred. Posing as a writer, photographer Tom Howard smuggled a tiny camera into the execution chamber, strapped to his ankle. When the switch was pulled, he is said to have raised his pant leg and triggered the shutter from a cable that ran up the inside of his pant leg and into his pocket. Papers reported that it took a total of seven minutes for Snyder to die. The image of Ruth Snyder was the first photograph of an execution at Sing Sing, a place that loomed large in the public imaginary (Buckland and Evans 16).

22. FBI historian Sanford Ungar notes that ever since it started keeping track of crime trends, the FBI has reported a steady increase (cited in Stabile, "Conspiracy" 271).

23. Hoover, who had always claimed to be apolitical, was keen to see Nixon elected. The 1960s had been difficult for Hoover, the Kennedy and Johnson administrations not nearly as enthusiastic about Hoover's approach to law and order as previous presidents had been. Robert F. Kennedy had gone so far as to identify the FBI as "a very dangerous organization" (Stabile, "Conspiracy" 267). To make matters more desperate, Hoover, approaching the age of mandatory retirement, was extremely reluctant to let go of the reins of power. His "paranoid, authoritarian personality" did not take well to the idea of retirement or to the highly visible antiauthoritarian practices of political protestors. Nor did Hoover appreciate the changing composition of the American public sphere during the 1960s, intentionally and systematically harassing and then failing to protect Dr. Martin Luther King from political assassination.

24. Carol Stabile argues that the increased media coverage of crime in the late 1960s cannot be divorced from the racist policies of Hoover's FBI during this time: "The crime wave that begins in the 1960s thus has its origins in a specifically white supremacist understanding of politics, political activism, and the role of people of color in U.S. society and in the racially motivated, highly coordinated government attack on people of color that followed from such understandings" ("Conspiracy" 267). Her research demonstrates that leading up to and following the 1968 election, news coverage of crime waves and calls for law and order were "consistently paired with pieces on political dissent" (272).

FIVE. *America's Most Wanted*

1. The program faced cancellation once in the 1990s but was brought back by popular demand. Low ratings at the turn of the century threatened cancellation again, but the terrorist attacks of Sept. 11, 2001, made the show highly relevant to viewers once again.

2. The show's format was initially a product of the severe economic constraints at its inception. John Thornton Caldwell argues that *AMW*'s bare-bones realism was not only an aesthetic produced by economic necessity, but a strategy developed by the show's producers to distinguish it from the high-production, high-gloss, highly stylized look of programs like *Miami Vice* (284). *AMW* embraced its cheap set and made it signify the televisual real in comparison to expensive crime dramas.

3. In the late 1980s the Reagan-appointed Federal Communications Commission passed a series of deregulatory initiatives aimed at stimulating a climate of aggressive competition that would break up the monopolies held by the three major networks. In this context Rupert Murdoch's News Corporation created the Fox Network. Facing the steep start-up costs required to compete with established networks, Fox developed reality cop shows as a strategy for breaking in on the networks' action. The new genre was extremely cheap in terms of production costs and demographically targeted (Williams 97–98; Pitman 171–72). By the mid-1990s making a single episode of a program like *AMW* cost approximately one-fourth what it did to produce a single sit-com episode and only one-half as much as a tabloid news-magazine (Pitman 172; Fishman 67).

4. Nielsen ratings suggest that *America's Most Wanted* tends to be watched more by women and the elderly, although the program retains a broad base of millions of viewers. According to Mark Fishman, reality crime shows do not reach huge audiences: "Their ratings and shares range from modest to poor" (71). Even so, he reminds us, they attract millions of viewers. Multiply millions by the number of years *America's Most Wanted* has been on the air, and it is fair to say that this program has exerted a significant influence on the visual culture of crime and punishment in America.

5. The law-and-order position advocates a minimalist function for the state. It reconstructs citizenship and the public sphere exclusively through the categories of law and order (Donovan 132–33).

6. See Oliver and Armstrong.

7. See http://www.crimestopusa.com. According to the Crime Stoppers Web site, "Crime Stoppers was the brainchild of a young Albuquerque detective who was concerned by the number of unsolved cases he and fellow detectives were working." He was particularly upset about the unsolved case of a murdered college student. He initiated a partnership among members of the local community, the media, and law enforcement and formed the first Crime Stoppers program on Sept. 8, 1976, offering a cash reward for anonymous tips leading to the arrest of the student's murderers.

Within seventy-two hours the case had been solved and the felons arrested (http://www.crimestopusa.com/AboutUs.asp#).

8. Such appeals dovetailed with the agenda of the National Rifle Association (NRA). The NRA had long been training both American law enforcement officials and ordinary citizens in the use of firearms. In the late twentieth century the NRA began offering instructional clinics like "Women on Target," which provides firearms training for women. In 2001 the NRA launched its "Refuse to Be a Victim" program, which trains seminar participants in avoidance strategies. A promotional video for the program clearly states its aim: "Refuse to Be a Victim is not about firearms; it's about planning your own personal safety strategy" (http://www.nra.org/aboutus.aspx). The video argues that the program is necessary because of the "increasing odds" of violent crime. The program's 2001 launch suggests that it is also concerned with issues of "preparedness" in the face of another terrorist attack.

9. See http://www.ncpc.org/about/history for the history of the NPCP. The 1980s were of course also the decade of America's "war on drugs," which similarly privileged the American child as its figure of innocence and vulnerability. One public service announcement circulated by the NCPC features McGruff playing a piano outdoors, surrounded by a bunch of friendly elementary school kids, who sing along with the crime dog's catchy tune: "Don't use drugs, don't use drugs." The privileged figure of innocence starring in the war on drugs was not just any American child, but specifically coded as white, middle-class, and suburban, in contrast to the war's imagined villains: nonwhite adult members of urban gangs (special episodes of *Different Strokes* starring Nancy Reagan notwithstanding).

10. For a brief period the show tried a more upbeat title sequence, which mixed images of the good life with images of crime and emergency (Episode 239). The music became more relaxed and jazzy, the scenes sunnier, and the new title sequence was edited at a significantly slower pace. A second, self-congratulatory montage followed this kinder, gentler opening sequence. Also accompanied by jazzy music, it has a behind-the-scenes feel. Its images include a police raid, phone calls, a guy in custody, police dogs, someone answering the phone at *AMW,* and a shot of guy with his shirt off giving the camera a thumbs-up. A man's voice says, "It's a damn good show, I mean, they caught me." This is followed by images of a woman giving the camera a thumbs-up and of a girl returned to her parents. A woman's voice says, "I can't believe they did it." Then the viewer sees a man in a prison uniform and cuffs who covers his face as a woman's voice says, "He'll never do it again." The sequence ends with a shot of a construction worker also giving the camera a thumbs-up. Within a year or less, however, the show was back to the fear-mongering approach of the original, high-stimulation title sequence.

11. Williams writes: "Anyone colored, of lower socioeconomic class or gay or lesbian are excluded from the domestic sphere even as victims. They get de facto positioned as victimizers" (110).

12. The show's success rate is undeniable and, quite frankly, astounding. By

Episode 163, the program claimed to have captured 148 fugitives—close to one per episode.

13. As of the writing of this chapter, *AMW* has captured over 1,000 fugitives.

14. *The Colbert Report* mocks the Fox Network and likely *AMW*'s graphic excesses. Interestingly, it also seems to pick up on *AMW*'s fake journalism. Long before *The Daily Show* premiered, *America's Most Wanted* portrayed John Walsh as if he were a news anchor. Like *The Daily Show*, *AMW* relies on "correspondents" to cover stories, although these individuals appear to be actors playing reporters, rather than trained journalists. In other words, *America's Most Wanted* was fake news before fake news was cool.

15. Pitman writes that the program's habit of displaying telephones and televisions on the set "serves to insert the televisual into the viewers' everyday lives" (173).

16. Donovan also argues that the show makes a populist appeal (125).

17. Anna Williams makes a similar argument, noting that the program consistently invokes the nation's capitol in order to signal that its information is "the most official and up to date" and as a means of "calling upon the political authority and respect due" to the federal government and the FBI (99).

18. The case of Patty Hearst and the Symbionese Liberation Army was a signal moment in the transition from outlaw to victim displays in U.S. visual cultures of crime and punishment. For an in-depth analysis of Hearst's unique status as missing and wanted, and the ways in which her gender performance troubled the conventional frames of guilt and innocence, see my essay "Patty and Me: Performative Encounters between an Historical Body and the History of Images."

19. Williams argues that Walsh's quick celebrity was facilitated by a wider 1980s trend "to connect men with children and discredit the claim that children's best interests were served by women" (113).

20. See signs of sexual abuse at http://www.sandf.org/articles/Signs.asp.

21. This type of exposure is reminiscent of the "wanted posters" issued for known abortion doctors by the pro-life movement during the 1990s.

22. The victims' rights movement was part of a broad move by conservatives for a return to "family values." There is a good deal of overlap, demographically and ideologically, between the victims' rights movement and the pro-life movement. The two privileged figures of American innocence during the 1980s and 1990s were the missing child and the aborted fetus. See Lauren Berlant's theory of infantile citizenship for a detailed discussion of the aborted fetus's role in American politics during these years. See also Stabile, "Shooting" for a discussion of fetal imagery in American visual culture.

23. Writing in 1998, Gray Cavender uses the phrase "us versus them" to describe *AMW*'s worldview and links this dynamic to the host's repeated and insistent use of the pronoun "we" (87).

24. There are also significant exceptions to this rule, where white actors are cast to play nonwhite victims so that the uniform whiteness of innocence in the world of *AMW* is preserved at the price of historical accuracy. For a brilliant discussion of one such case, see Pitman.

25. McDowell raises a crucial question: is it possible to lionize victims without leaving their images open to symbolic exploitation? The politics of exposure, which motivates a good deal of journalistic and documentary image-making, assumes that showing the public what's wrong with the world today will generate empathy and social reform. But McDowell goes on to say, "as images supposedly used to 'open our eyes' to the face of black death, to ignite a national discussion about the urgency of 'saving' the lives of young black men, these post-mortems would seem instead to habituate the public to the inevitable reality of their deaths, rendering them 'natural' and 'unnatural' all at once" (167).

Conclusion

1. William J. T. Mitchell argues that the iconic image of the World Trade Center signifies not only the destruction of the Twin Towers but also, and perhaps more frighteningly, "the potential for the destruction of images in our time, a new and more virulent form of iconoclasm" (13).

2. See Conquergood: "The ritual replaying of traditional form always plays with, and plays off and against, the performance genealogy that it recites" (343).

3. Marita Sturken's recent study of nationalist kitsch and consumerism after 9/11 reveals how Americans literally bought into patriotism, performing American innocence through repeated acts of purchase and spending (*Tourists*).

4. The televised execution of Timothy McVeigh is an important precursor. However, that event differs sharply from the Hussein execution in that American legal authorities tightly controlled the media event, whereas the second video was "accidentally" made public. For a detailed analysis of the McVeigh execution, see Sturken, *Tourists*.

5. See Sontag; Brison.

6. Two hundred of these flyers were collected and framed to comprise a traveling exhibition entitled "Missing: Last Seen at the World Trade Center on September 11, 2001."

7. Charged with the open question of whether those pictured were still alive or already dead, the missing notices offered powerful images of uncertainty. Jones, Zagacki, and Lewis describe the texts as "affirmative performative enactments of uncertainty" (115). Drawing on the work of Kennerly, who writes about roadside shrines, Jones et al. point out the liminal status of the missing notices, which marked a "space between the moment when a missing person was last known to be alive and before that person was acknowledged to be dead. . . . They 'froze' time and

transformed the liminal period so that people looking for their lost loved ones could keep hoping, avoid shock, and resist the urge to dwell on the very distinct possibility that the missing person was already dead, already vanished into the past" (108).

8. Some of the best studies of 9/11 and photographic practices adopt a psychoanalytic framework in order to explore photography's formal resonance with traumatic experience and memory. These analyses privilege the individual over the collective or apply theories of individual trauma to the collective. Marianne Hirsch writes: "To photograph is to look in a different way—to look without understanding. Understanding is deferred until we see the developed image. Deferral connects photography to trauma, which is characterized by delayed understanding, and so perhaps photography can help us understand the traumatic effects of September 11" ("Day" 2). Barbie Zelizer writes: "Personal response marks the process of recovering from trauma. Individuals experiencing trauma tend to respond first in individuated states connected to personal roles—as parents, children or spouses—even when asked to activate professional roles in connection with trauma at hand. A space is created by which individuals work through the encounter with trauma first as individuals and only afterward as members of a broader collective" ("Finding" 698).

9. "Guard and Reserves Define 'Spirit of America': Remarks by the President to Employees at the Pentagon" (http://www.whitehouse.gov/news/releases/2001/09/20010917-3.html, accessed Oct. 14, 2004).

10. In a press conference held by President Bush on General Pervez Musharraf's "frontier strategy" in Pakistan, he said, "This is wild country—this is wilder than the Wild West." He also stated that he knew Musharraf was on the side of the Americans because the terrorists had tried to kill him (BBC, Feb. 2007). President Bush was also quoted making a similar statement on the PBS *News Hour:* "This is wild country. Wilder than the Wild West" (Feb. 26, 2007).

11. For a detailed discussion of media representations of Saddam Hussein's capture, see R. Hall, "Ziploc."

12. The American public has not always been so cooperative. Political opponents of the Bush Administration quickly followed suit by issuing mock decks like the "Regime Change" playing cards, which call for the capture and arrest of key figures in the conservative administration. Likewise, cultural authorities like David Letterman cleverly lampooned the "playing" cards. On Oct. 31, 2003, for example, Letterman dressed a child actor up in a Saddam Hussein playing card Halloween costume (Episode 2067). This stunt mocks the Pentagon's mock wanted poster for Saddam Hussein by making it into a white child's costume. The wanted poster's gesture of masking state violence with the bogeyman Hussein is thereby unmasked. The humor of the gag comes from the wanted poster's historic service to racist presumptions regarding who is innocent and who is guilty.

13. This is merely one instance among many in which the Bush Administration has encouraged or at least agreed to ignore a degree of vigilantism as good for the health of the party. Other examples include bounty hunters who traveled to Afghani-

stan to bring Bin Laden back, dead or alive, and the Minuteman Civil Defense Corps, a voluntary organization of U.S. citizens who stand as armed guards at the border between the United States and Mexico.

14. For examples of vernacular posters see http://ebtx.com/wtc/osamwant.htm, http://hereisnewyork.org/index2.asp.

15. Talk given at the annual meeting of the American Political Science Association in 2006.

BIBLIOGRAPHY

Agamben, Georgio. *Homo Sacer: Sovereign Power and Bare Life*. Stanford: Stanford University Press, 1998.

——. *State of Exception*. Chicago: University of Chicago Press, 2005.

Allen, James, Jon Lewis, Leon F. Litwack, and Hilton Als. *Without Sanctuary: Lynching Photography in America*. Santa Fe: Twin Palms, 2000.

Anderson, Patricia. *The Printed Image and the Transformation of Popular Culture, 1790–1860*. London: Oxford University Press, 1991.

Bachelard, Gaston. *The Poetics of Space*. Trans. Maria Jolas. Boston: Beacon Press, 1994.

Barthes, Roland. *Camera Lucida: Reflections on Photography*. New York: Hill and Wang, 1981.

Batchen, Geoffrey. *Each Wild Idea: Writing, Photography, History*. Boston: MIT Press, 2001.

Beckman, Karen. "Terrorism, Feminism, Sisters, and Twins: Building Relations in the Wake of the World Trade Center Attacks." *Grey Room* 7 (Spring 2002): 24–39.

Benjamin, Walter. *The Arcades Project*. Ed. Rolf Tiedemann. New York: Belknap, 2002.

——. *Illuminations*. New York: Harcourt, 1968.

——. *Reflections: Essays, Aphorisms, Autobiographical Writings*. New York: Harcourt Brace Jovanovich, 1978.

——. *The Writer of Modern Life: Essays on Charles Baudelaire*. Ed. M. W. Jennings. Cambridge: Harvard University Press, 2006.

Bennett, Tony. *The Birth of the Museum: History, Theory, Politics*. New York: Routledge, 1995.

"Bergdoll Family Papers Register." Philadelphia: Balch Institute for Ethnic Studies of the Historical Society of Pennsylvania, 1974.

Berlant, Lauren. *The Queen of America Goes to Washington City: Essays on Sex and Citizenship*. Durham: Duke University Press, 1997.

Bowman, Michael. "Killing Dillinger: A Mystory." *Text and Performance Quarterly* 20, no. 4 (2000): 342–74.

Brison, Susan. "Torture or 'Good Old American Pornography'?" *Chronicle Review,* June 4, 2004.

Brown, Claudine K. "Mug Shot: Suspicious Person." Willis 137–43.

Brown, Steven E. "Sexuality and the Slave Community." *Phylon* 42, no. 1 (1981): 1–10.

Buckland, Gail, and Harold Evans. *Shots in the Dark: True Crime Pictures.* Boston: Little, Brown, 2001.

Butler, Judith. *Precarious Life: The Powers of Mourning and Violence.* New York: Verso, 2003.

Byrnes, Thomas. *1886 Professional Criminals of America.* New York: Lyons Press, 2000.

Caldwell, John Thornton. *Televisuality: Style, Crisis, and Authority in American Television.* New Brunswick: Rutgers University Press, 1995.

Campbell, Karlyn Kohrs. *Man Cannot Speak for Her.* New York: Greenwood Press, 1995.

Carby, Hazel. "On the Threshold." *Critical Inquiry* 12, no. 1 (1985): 262–77.

Carens, Joseph H. *Democracy and Possessive Individualism: The Intellectual Legacy of C. B. Macpherson.* Albany: State University of New York Press, 1993.

Carey, James W. *Communication as Culture: Essays on Media and Society.* Boston: Unwin Hyman, 1989.

Castiglia, Christopher. *Bound and Determined: Captivity, Culture-Crossing, and White Womanhood from Mary Rowlandson to Patty Hearst.* Chicago: University of Chicago Press, 1996.

Cavender, Gray. "In 'The Shadow of Shadows': Television Reality Crime Programming." Fishman and Cavender 79–94.

Charney, Leo, and Vanessa Schwartz, eds. *Cinema and the Invention of Modern Life.* Berkeley: University of California Press, 1995.

Clark, Elizabeth. "'The Sacred Rights of the Weak': Pain, Sympathy, and the Culture of Individual Rights in Antebellum America." *Journal of American History* 82 (1995): 463–93.

Clark, Sarah. *Women and Crime in the Street Literature of Early Modern England.* New York: Palgrave Macmillan, 2003.

Cloud, Dana. "'To Veil the Threat of Terror': Afghan Women and the 'Clash of Civilizations' in the Imagery of the U.S. War on Terrorism." *Quarterly Journal of Speech* 90, no. 3 (2004): 285–306.

Cohen, Daniel A. *Pillars of Salt, Monuments of Grace: New England Crime Literature and the Origins of American Popular Culture, 1674–1860.* Amherst: University of Massachusetts Press, 2006.

Cohn, Bernard S. *Colonialism and Its Forms of Knowledge: The British in India.* Princeton: Princeton University Press, 1996.

Cole, Simon A. *Suspect Identities: A History of Fingerprinting and Criminal Identification.* Cambridge: Harvard University Press, 2001.

Collins, Kathleen. "Portraits of Slave Children." *History of Photography* 9, no. 3 (1985): 187–210.

Collison, Robert Lewis. *The Story of Street Literature: Forerunner of the Popular Press*. London: Dent, 1973.

Conquergood, Dwight. "Lethal Theatre: Performance, Punishment, and the Death Penalty." *Theatre Journal* 54 (2002): 339–67.

Crowther, M. Anne. "The History of Crime and Punishment in Britain 1790–1870: 'Hanging Ballads' and Sensational Literature." Glasgow: University of Glasgow, 1999. http://special.lib.gla.ac.uk/teach/hang/intro.html. Accessed February 2007.

Davis, A. "Afro Images: Politics, Fashion, and Nostalgia." Willis 171–79.

Davis, Adrienne. "The Sexual Economy of American Slavery." Talk. University of North Carolina, Chapel Hill, February 25, 2003.

Debord, Guy. *Society of the Spectacle*. Detroit: Black & Red, 1973.

De Certeau, Michel. *Practices of Everyday Life*. Berkeley: University of California Press, 2002.

Deleuze, Gilles, and Felix Guattari. *A Thousand Plateaus: Capitalism and Schizophrenia*. Minneapolis: University of Minnesota Press, 1987.

Derrida, Jacques. "Force of Law." *Cardoza Law Review* 11 (1990): 919–86.

Didion, Joan. "Girl of the Golden West." *After Henry*. New York: Vintage International, 1992. 95–109.

Donovan, Pamela. "Armed with the Power of Television: Reality Crime Programming and the Reconstruction of Law and Order in the United States." Fishman and Cavender 117–37.

Douglas, Ann. *The Feminization of American Culture*. New York: Farrar, Straus and Giroux, 1998.

Douglas, Mary. *Purity and Danger: An Analysis of the Concepts of Pollution and Taboo*. New York: Routledge, 1992.

Dove, Donna J., and Jeffrey M. Maynard. *FBI's Ten Most Wanted Fugitives Program: 50th Anniversary 1950–2000*. Lisbon, Md.: K & D Limited, Inc., 2000.

Edgerton, Samuel Y. *Pictures and Punishment: Art and Criminal Prosecution during the Florentine Renaissance*. Ithaca: Cornell University Press, 1985.

Ehrenhaus, Peter, and Susan Owen. "Race Lynching and Christian Evangelicalism: Performances of Faith." *Text and Performance Quarterly* 24, nos. 3–4 (2004): 276–301.

Enloe, Cynthia. "The Gendered Gulf." *Collateral Damage: The "New World Order" at Home and Abroad*. Ed. C. Peters. Boston: South End, 1992. 93–110.

Farrell, Thomas, and Tamar Katriel. "Scrapbooks as Cultural Texts: An American Art of Memory." *Text and Performance Quarterly* 11, no. 1 (1991): 1–17.

Feldman, Allen. "From Desert Storm to Rodney King via Ex-Yugoslavia: On Cultural Anesthesia." *The Senses Still: Perception and Memory as Material Culture in Modernity.* Ed. Nadia Seremetakis. Chicago: University of Chicago Press, 1996. 87–108.

Fishman, Mark. "Ratings and Reality: The Persistence of the Reality Crime Genre." Fishman and Cavender 59–75.

Fishman, Mark, and Gray Cavender, eds. *Entertaining Crime: Television Reality Programs.* New York: Aldine de Gruyter, 1998.

Flynn, Steven. *America the Vulnerable: How Our Government Is Failing to Protect Us from Terrorism.* New York: Harper, 2005.

Foucault, Michel. *Discipline and Punish: The Birth of the Prison.* New York: Vintage Books, 1995.

——. "The Eye of Power." *Power/Knowledge: Selected Interviews and Other Writings.* Ed. Colin Gordon. New York: Pantheon, 1980. 146–65.

Fuoss, Kirk. "Lynching Performances, Theatres of Violence." *Text and Performance Quarterly* 19, no. 1 (1999): 1–37.

Garber, Marjorie. *Sex and Real Estate: Why We Love Homes.* New York: Anchor Books, 2001.

Gaylor, Edwin S. Letter to Robert Pinkerton. Philadelphia, 1894.

Ginzburg, Carlo. "Clues: Morelli, Freud, and Sherlock Holmes." *The Sign of Three: Dupin, Holmes, Peirce.* Ed. Umberto Eco and Thomas A. Sebeok. Bloomington: Indiana University Press, 1983. 81–118.

Gitlin, Todd. *Inside Prime Time.* New York: Pantheon, 1983.

Green-Lewis, Jennifer. *Framing the Victorians: Photography and the Culture of Realism.* Ithaca: Cornell University Press, 1996.

Gunning, Tom. "Tracing the Individual Body: Body, Photography, Detectives, and Early Cinema." Charney and Schwartz 15–45.

Hall, Jacquelyn Dowd. "The Mind That Burns Each Body." *Powers of Desire.* Ed. Ann Snitow, Christine Stansell, and Sharon Thompson. New York: Monthly Review Press, 1983. 328–49.

Hall, Rachel. "Missing Dolly, Mourning Slavery: The Slave Notice as Keepsake." *Camera Obscura: Feminism, Culture, and Media Studies* 61 (April 2006): 71–103.

——. "Of Ziploc Bags and Black Holes: The Aesthetics of Transparency in the War on Terror." *Communication Review* 10 (2007): 319–46.

——. "Patty and Me: Performative Encounters between an Historical Body and the History of Images." *Text and Performance Quarterly* 26, no. 4 (2006): 347–70.

Hall, Stuart, Charles Critcher, Tony Jefferson, and John Clarke. *Policing the Crisis: Mugging, the State, and Law and Order.* Hampshire: Palgrave Macmillan, 1978.

Harris, Joseph. *The Ballad and Oral Literature.* Cambridge: Harvard University Press, 1991.

Hawkins, William. "Lunsford Lane; or, Another Helper from North Carolina." *Documenting the American South.* Chapel Hill, 1863.

Hearst, Patricia, and A. Moscow. *Every Secret Thing.* Garden City, N.Y.: Doubleday, 1982.

Henkin, David M. *City Reading: Written Words and Public Spaces in Antebellum New York.* New York: Columbia University Press, 1998.

Henning, Michelle. "The Subject as Object: Photography and the Human Body." Wells 217–50.

Hirsch, Marianne. "The Day Time Stopped." *Chronicle of Higher Education,* January 25, 2002.

——, ed. *The Familial Gaze.* Hanover: Dartmouth College Press, 1999.

——. *Family Frames: Photography, Narrative, and Postmemory.* Cambridge: Harvard University Press, 1997.

Hobsbawm, Eric J. *Bandits.* New York: New Press, 2000.

Holdzkom, R. "Manigault Family Papers Inventory." Chapel Hill: Southern Historical Collection, Wilson Library, University of North Carolina, 1990.

Holland, Patricia. " 'Sweet It Is to Scan': Personal Photographs and Popular Photography." Wells 117–64.

Hoover, J. Edgar. "Criminal Identification." *Annals of the American Academy of Political and Social Science* 146 (1929): 205–13.

Hopkins, D. "Weegee and Warhol: Voyeurism, Shock and the Discourse on Criminality." *History of Photography* 25, no. 4 (2001): 357–67.

"How to Take Finger Prints." Prepared by the Identification Division, U.S. Department of Justice. *American City,* March 1928, 117–19.

Isenberg, Nancy. "Not 'Anyone's Daughter': Patty Hearst and the Postmodern Legal Subject." *American Quarterly* 52, no. 4 (2000): 639–81.

Ivy, M. "Have You Seen Me? Recovering the Inner Child in Late Twentieth-Century America." *Social Text* 37 (Winter 1993): 227–52.

Jameson, Frederic. *Postmodernism; or, The Cultural Logic of Late Capitalism.* Durham: Duke University Press, 1991.

Jay, Martin. *Downcast Eyes: The Denigration of Vision in Twentieth-Century French Thought.* Berkeley: University of California Press, 1993.

Jeffords, Susan. "Rape and the New World Order." *Cultural Critique* 19 (Fall 1991): 203–15.

Jones, K. T., K. S. Zagacki, and T. Lewis. "Communication, Liminality, and Hope: The September 11th Missing Person Posters." *Communication Studies* 58 (2007): 105–21.

Kennerly, Rebecca. "Getting Messy: In the Field and at the Crossroads with Roadside Shrines." *Text and Performance Quarterly* 22, no. 4 (2002): 229–60.

Kumar, Amitava. *Passport Photos.* Berkeley: University of California Press, 2000.

Labinjoh, J. "The Sexual Life of the Oppressed: An Examination of the Family Life of Antebellum Slaves." *Phylon* 35, no. 4 (1974): 375–97.

Laqueur, Thomas. "Bodies, Details and the Humanitarian Narrative." *The New*

Cultural History. Ed. Lynn Hunt. Berkeley: University of California Press, 1989. 176–204.

Lefebvre, Henri. *Everyday Life in the Modern World*. Piscataway, N.J.: Transaction Publishers, 1984.

Lucas, Peter. "The Missing Person Photos." *Scholar and Feminist Online* 2, no. 1 (2003).

Luster, Deborah. *One Big Self: Prisoners of Louisiana*. Santa Fe: Twin Palms, 2003.

Manigault, Louis. "Family Album: 1856–1877." Chapel Hill: Southern Historical Collection, Wilson Library, University of North Carolina.

———. "Wartime Journal: 1861–1868." Chapel Hill: Southern Historical Collection, Wilson Library, University of North Carolina.

Marchand, Roland. *Advertising the American Dream: Making Way for Modernity, 1920–1940*. Berkeley: University of California Press, 1985.

Marien, Mary Warner. *Photography: A Cultural History*. Upper Saddle River, N.J.: Prentice Hall, 2002.

Marvin, Carolyn. *When Old Technologies Were New: Thinking about Electric Communication in the Late Nineteenth Century*. New York: Oxford University Press, 1988.

Marvin, Carolyn, and D. W. Ingle. *Blood Sacrifice and the Nation: Totem Rituals and the American Flag*. New York: Cambridge University Press, 1999.

Massumi, Brian. *The Politics of Everyday Fear*. Minneapolis: University of Minnesota Press, 1993.

McCauley, Elizabeth Anne. *A. A. E. Disdéri and the Carte de Visite Portrait Photograph*. New Haven: Yale University Press, 1985.

McDowell, Deborah E. "Viewing the Remains: A Polemic on Death, Spectacle, and the [Black] Family." Hirsch 153–77.

McElderry, M. "Pinkerton's National Detective Agency Finding Aid." Washington, D.C.: Manuscript Division, Library of Congress, 2001.

Meaders, Daniel. "South Carolina Fugitives as Viewed through Local Colonial Newspapers with Emphasis on Runaway Notices 1732–1801." *Journal of Negro History* 60, no. 2 (1975): 288–319.

Metz, Christian. "Photography and Fetish." *October* 34 (1985): 81–90.

Meyer, Richard. *Outlaw Representation: Censorship and Homosexuality in Twentieth-Century American Art*. Boston: Beacon Press, 2002.

Meyer, Richard E. "The Outlaw: A Distinctive American Folktype." *Journal of the Folklore Institute* 17 (1980): 94–124.

Michaelson, Mark, Steven Kasher, and Bob Nickas. *Least Wanted*. New York: Steidl/Steven Kasher Gallery, 2006.

Miller, Nancy K. " 'Portraits of Grief': Telling Details and the Testimony of Trauma." *Differences: A Journal of Feminist Cultural Studies* 14, no. 3 (2003): 112–35.

Mitchell, Mary N. " 'Rosebloom and Pure White,' or So It Seemed." *American Quarterly* 54, no. 3 (2002): 369–410.

Mitchell, William J. T. *What Do Pictures Want? The Lives and Loves of Images.* Chicago: University of Chicago Press, 2005.

Morn, Frank. *"The Eye That Never Sleeps": A History of the Pinkerton National Detective Agency.* Bloomington: Indiana University Press, 1982.

Newhall, Beaumont. *The History of Photography.* 5th ed. New York: Museum of Modern Art, 1999.

Nichols, Bill. *Representing Reality: Issues and Concepts in Documentary.* Bloomington: Indiana University Press, 1991.

Oliver, Mary Beth, and G. Blake Armstrong. "The Color of Crime: Perceptions of Caucasians and African Americans' Involvement in Crime." Fishman and Cavender 19–35.

Phillips, Sandra S. *Police Pictures: The Photograph as Evidence.* San Francisco: Chronicle Books, 1997.

Pinkerton, Allen. *General Principles.* 1st ed. New York: Jones Printing Company, 1878.

"Pinkerton History." *Pinkerton Burns Website.* http://www.pinkertons.com/com panyinfo/history/pinkertons/history—sleep.asp. Accessed February 12, 2003.

Pinkerton's National Detective Agency. Records. Washington, D.C.: Manuscript Division, Library of Congress.

Pitman, Barbara A. "Re-mediating the Spaces of Reality Television: *America's Most Wanted* and the Case of Vancouver's Missing Women." *Environment and Planning A* 34 (2001): 167–84.

"Post." Definition. *Oxford English Dictionary.* 2nd ed. 1989.

Potter, Claire B. *War on Crime: Bandits, G-Men, and the Politics of Mass Culture.* New Brunswick: Rutgers University Press, 1998.

Raiford, Leigh. "The Consumption of Lynching Images." *Only Skin Deep: Changing Visions of the American Self.* Ed. Coco Fusco and Brian Wallis. New York: Harry N. Abrams, 2003. 267–74.

Roach, Joseph R. *Cities of the Dead: Circum-Atlantic Performance.* New York: Columbia University Press, 1996.

Ruby, Jay. *Secure the Shadow: Death and Photography in America.* Cambridge: MIT Press, 1995.

Ruth, David. *Inventing the Public Enemy: The Gangster in American Culture, 1918–1934.* Chicago: University of Chicago Press, 1996.

Sayre, Henry M. *The Object of Performance: The American Avant-Garde since 1970.* Chicago: University of Chicago Press, 1989.

Sconce, Jeffrey. "XXX: Love and Kisses from Charlie." *Swinging Single: Representing Sexuality in the 1960s.* Ed. H. Radner and M. Tucker. Minneapolis: University of Minnesota Press, 1989. 207–23.

Sedgwick, Eve Kosofsky. *Tendencies.* Durham: Duke University Press, 1993.

Sekula, Allan. "The Body and the Archive." *October* 39 (1986): 1–64.

Simon, Taryn. *The Innocents.* Brooklyn: Umbrage Editions, 2003.

Sontag, Susan. "Regarding the Torture of Others." *New York Times Magazine,* May 23, 2004.

Southern Sources: An Exhibition Celebrating Seventy-Five Years of the Southern Historical Collection, 1930–2005. Chapel Hill: University of North Carolina University Library, 2005.

Stabile, Carol. "Conspiracy or Consensus? Reconsidering the Moral Panic." *Journal of Communication Inquiry* 25, no. 3 (2001): 258–78.

———. "Shooting the Mother: Fetal Photography and the Politics of Disappearance." Treichler, Cartwright, and Penley 171–97.

———. *White Victims, Black Villains: Gender, Race and Crime News in U.S. Culture.* New York: Routledge, 2006.

Steedman, Carolyn. *Dust: The Archive and Cultural History.* New Brunswick: Rutgers University Press, 2002.

———. *Strange Dislocations: Childhood and the Idea of Human Interiority, 1780–1930.* Cambridge: Harvard University Press, 1995.

Stewart, Susan. *On Longing: Narratives of the Miniature, the Gigantic, the Souvenir, the Collection.* Durham: Duke University Press, 1993.

Storr, Robert, and Gerhard Richter. *Gerhard Richter: October 18, 1977.* New York: Museum of Modern Art, 2002.

Straw, Will. *Cyanide and Sin: Visualizing Crime in 50s America.* New York: PPP Editions, 2006.

Sturken, Marita. "The Aesthetics of Absence: Rebuilding Ground Zero." *American Ethnologist* 31, no. 3 (2004): 311–25.

———. "The Image as Memorial." Hirsch 178–95.

———. *Tourists of History: Memory, Kitsch, and Consumerism from Oklahoma City to Ground Zero.* Durham: Duke University Press, 2007.

Tagg, John. *The Burden of Representation: Essays on Photographies and Histories.* Minneapolis: University of Minnesota Press, 1993.

Trachtenberg, Alan. *Reading American Photographs: Images as History, Mathew Brady to Walker Evans.* New York: Hill and Wang, 1989.

Treichler, P. A., L. Cartwright, and C. Penley, eds. *The Visible Woman: Imaging Technologies, Gender, and Science.* New York: New York University Press, 1998.

Turner, Victor. *From Ritual to Theatre: The Human Seriousness of Play.* New York: PAJ Publications, 1982.

———. "Images of Anti-Temporality: An Essay in the Anthropology of Experience." *Harvard Theological Review* 75, no. 2 (1982): 243–65.

"Urgent Need for Greater Efficiency in Criminal Identification." *American City,* March 1928, 116–17.

Verhagen, Marcus. "The Poster in *Fin-de-siècle* Paris: 'That Mobile and Degenerate Art.'" Charney and Schwartz 103–29.

Weiler, Jonathan, and M. J. Hetherington. "Authoritarianism and the American

Political Divide." *Democratic Strategist: A Journal of Public Opinion & Political Strategy* (2006).

Wells, L., ed. *Photography: A Critical Introduction.* New York: Routledge, 2001.

White, Hayden. *The Content of the Form: Narrative Discourse and Historical Representation.* Baltimore: Johns Hopkins University Press, 1987.

White, R. "Outlaw Gangs of the Middle Border: American Social Bandits." *Western Historical Quarterly* 12 (1981): 387–408.

Wiegman, Robyn. *American Anatomies: Theorizing Race and Gender.* Durham: Duke University Press, 1995.

Wigley, Mark. "Untitled: The Housing of Gender." *Sexuality and Space.* Ed. Beatriz Colomina. New York: Princeton Architectural Press, 1992. 327–89.

Williams, Anna. "Domestic Violence and the Aetiology of Crime in *America's Most Wanted.*" *Camera Obscura: A Journal of Feminism and Film Theory* 31 (1993): 97–118.

Williamson, Judith. "Family, Education, Photography." *Culture/Power/History: A Reader in Contemporary Social Theory.* Ed. N. B. Dirks, G. Eley, and S. B. Ortner. Princeton: Princeton University Press, 1994. 236–44.

Willis, Deborah, ed. *Picturing Us: African American Identity in Photography.* New York: New Press, 1994.

Willis, Deborah, and Carla Williams. *The Black Female Body: A Photographic History.* Philadelphia: Temple University Press, 2002.

Zelizer, Barbie. "Finding Aids to the Past: Bearing Personal Witness to Traumatic Public Events." *Media, Culture and Society* 24, no. 5 (2002): 697–714.

——. "The Voice of the Visual in Memory." *Framing Public Memory.* Ed. K. R. Phillips. Tuscaloosa: University of Alabama Press, 2002. 157–86.

Index

abolitionists, 53–57

Abu Ghraib, 139, 146

Adam and *Adam: His Song Continues* (films), 122

African Americans: on *America's Most Wanted*, 111, 114, 127; *Dying Confession of Pomp, a Negro Man,* 31–32, *32;* lynching, 18–19, 62–63; mug shots as disciplining, 50, 60–62, *61. See also* slaves

Agamben, Georgio, 13, 152, 165n11

Agassiz, Louis, 51, 53

Alton, Ill., execution, 41

American City (magazine), 98

American Journal of Photography, 65–66

America's Most Wanted (television program), 110–35; audience of, 168n4; corporate sponsors of, 130–31; cost to produce, 168n3; crime as symbolic threat on, 114; Crime Stoppers as partner of, 112; criminals caught as result of, 7, 115, 169n12, 170n13; disparity between number of calls and useful information, 112; dramatic reenactments of crimes on, 123–24, 126–27, 128; emotionalism of, 118, 125; FBI in production of, 110, 111; fugitive and victim display juxtaposed on, 21–22, 126; gendering of law enforcement on, 119; hybrid of masculine and feminine addresses in, 122–23; law enforcement as portrayed on, 111, 128–29; missing children on, 126–28; paternal relationship to viewers of, 119; populist address of, 118; privatization of fugitive display in, 21, 121–22; social context of emergence of, 21, 112; as televisual community policing, 111–13; tips for avoiding violent crime, 125–26; "us versus them" worldview of, 127, 170n23; victims on, 114, 118, 121–26, 127; viewer participation in, 111–12; vigilante viewers of, 6, 8, 109, 120; Washington headquarters of, 116, 170n17; white empowerment promised by, 114; women's and children's narratives of victimization on, 122–25

Anderson, Patricia, 31

anthropological portraits, 50–51, 53, 138

antiglobalization movement, 150

armed robbery, 96

auto theft, 97, 99, 101

Awful Beacon to the Rising Generation, The, 34–37, *36*

Bain, George Grantham, 163n22

Barrow, Clyde, *103,* 105

Barthes, Roland, 143

Batchen, Geoffrey, 15

Benjamin, Walter, 14, 79, 160n18, 164n4